The Clueless Project Manager

The Clueless Project Manager

A Case of Project Management Reality

Abhay V. Trivedi, Ph. D.

authorHOUSE®

AuthorHouse™
1663 Liberty Drive
Bloomington, IN 47403
www.authorhouse.com
Phone: 1-800-839-8640

First published by AuthorHouse   10/12/2011
ISBN: 978-1-4670-6191-9 (sc)
ISBN: 978-1-4670-6190-2 (hc)
ISBN: 978-1-4670-6198-8 (ebk)

Library of Congress Control Number: 2011918306

Printed in the United States of America

Any people depicted in stock imagery provided by Thinkstock are models, and such images are being used for illustrative purposes only.
Certain stock imagery © Thinkstock.

This book is printed on acid-free paper.

CONTENTS

To my wife Shilpa
and the three boys Neil, Nikhil and Adi

THE SETUP

The intra terminal shuttle at the world's busiest airport was on strike. It was the Friday before the Fourth of July weekend and the airport was chaos. I was running as fast as I could to catch the last flight to Los Angeles. It was not a smart move. I took a tumble. Overweight and out of shape I could barely walk let alone do an end run through the crowd. As I lay flat, watching the beautiful ceiling of the airport, a sign flashed by my eyes—"last call to Los Angeles." I thanked my lucky stars. It could have been worse. All those people in a hurry could have trampled me. I had recently read that the airport was *the* place to vent and there were plenty of frustrated people around.

My whole life was a total mess, but Fridays were generally good to me, signaling the end of the work week and unwinding at the local watering hole. I had disciplined myself to absolute abstinence from any intelligent activity on Fridays. This Friday however was shaping up to be different. Instead of my regular "night at the bar" my boss had me flying to meet him in Los Angeles for an important Saturday meeting.

The thought of spending an entire weekend with a sixty year old recently divorced and pretty much arrogant and selfish man was not exciting. The thought of missing the flight was even worse.

Robert Frost III was my boss. He also owned the company. As far as I knew he was the baddest man in the whole darn South. The last time I had missed a meeting Mr. Frost had me assigned to Crexton, Ohio, a place so depressing even the mayor had to be motivated to stay in town.

The Fit-Food company had been my humble abode for the past many years. Our mission at Fit-Food was to maximize profits by minimizing quality. When you make food for the obese you needn't worry about quality. This demographic is happy to oblige at the sight of any food in front of them.

There were some definite perks working for the Fit-Food company. One of them was meeting celebrities who regularly advertised our diet products. The celebrities who advertised for Fit-Food, however, were known only in the South, where anyone with a full set of teeth is generally considered a celebrity. Most of our celebrities worked for NASCAR as tire changers. In this neck of the woods most would recognize NASCAR tire changers but not the Governor. You can't blame the people, though; most of our governors have a branch office in South America or Europe where they conduct most of their affairs anyway.

The Fit-Food company was in the right place at the right time. The demand for diet food had skyrocketed in the past decade. Fit-Food was flourishing. Mr. Frost, as he liked to be called by all of his employees, was the sole owner of

Fit-Food. He had inherited the company from his father, who killed himself in fear of seeing his only son destroy his legacy.

Mr. Frost had no clue how to run the weight loss business; he didn't have to. As long as there were Waffle Houses in the South the business was recession-proof or idiot-proof. The weight loss business was like the computer industry of the eighties; a lot of hype and a lot of mediocrity, however, both made you money.

The Fit-Food brand was recognized as one of the most powerful names in the South. The "Fit-Food" name was recognized by more people in the South than the "Swoosh" in Beaverton, Oregon. In fact, the "Swoosh" in the South was referred to as a carbonated drink. It doesn't take much of a genius to recognize why the South had lost the war

The Fit-Food company employed over a thousand employees, mostly in a volunteer capacity. They worked over sixty hours a week, but got paid as volunteers. They were promised excellent benefits after they served the company for twenty years. The hope was that after twenty years of hard labor they would not need any benefits. No wonder Mr. Frost's reading list only consisted of Mao Tse Tung's *Philosophies on Humanity.*

Some of us at Fit-Food fell in the category of project managers. A project manager at Fit-Food was defined as someone with a whole lot of responsibility and a much greater probability of getting fired with every project. Mr. Frost had read somewhere that anyone who had read "The Seven Habits of Smart People" was a certified project manager. I was one of the first project managers Mr. Frost had hired. I had the book in my hand during the interview. Mr. Frost believed in hiring the least qualified person at the lowest salary.

The first question Mr. Frost always asked his interviewees was, "What is the lowest salary you would accept?"

No wonder we had the most unqualified workforce in the entire South. Most of them I believe were ex-Waffle House employees or their cousins. I realized living in the South, the word cousin referred to everyone. Everyone was somehow related.

Recently Fit-Food had embarked upon a revolutionary idea of selling diet food. Mr. Frost had created a new line of "green" diet products, targeted at the new generation of "politically correct" obese people. The sight of politically correct obese people scared the daylights out of me, but it worked. The politically correct psychos had concluded that a cow packed in a green box made it holy and healthy to eat.

As the project manager for the "green" product lines, I was well aware of the requirements capture process from the stakeholders. In Fit-Food's case we had only one real stakeholder Mr. Frost. In a requirements gathering interview session he had commanded that the "green" line had to have all products packed in a green carton. The inside didn't matter. Mr. Frost had figured that the best way to fool the already food deprived customer was to color all the food cartons green. If the customer got too hungry he would eat the carton considering it to be another vegetable.

My years with the Fit-Food company and Mr. Frost had convinced me that America did not need innovators to succeed. It needed employers who could get the most out of any employee under any given situation. For the number of hours that Mr. Frost made me work I was making less money per hour than the Chinese worker in Shanghai or Kim Jong's barber.

My seniority at the Fit-Food company had earned me the respect of fellow project managers. I was also the only one with a full set of teeth. None of the project managers at Fit-Food had any clue on running projects. Some did have significant skills in running from the law.

At Fit-Food there were twenty designated project managers. Of those twenty project managers none had a technical degree. I was the closest to a technical genius with a degree in History. I was trained in the art of war. My buddies Timmy and Marcus had degrees in Physical Education and we were still waiting for the transcripts of Jay, Suzy and Denny for the past five years to confirm if they ever graduated from high school let alone college.

At Fit-Food we did not have a PMO. In fact we did not have an office. All project managers sat in the warehouse area with the forklifts zipping by at around 40 miles an hour. No wonder most NASCAR drivers came from the South. I was glad at Fit-Food we did not have the "bring your child to work day." The only time we were allowed to sit in an office was during the safety inspections.

The safety inspectors were generally bribed and they drove through the facility in Mr. Frost's ATV.

As a reward of my complete loyalty to Mr. Frost, I was also the head of the project manager's group (PMG) at Fit-Food. I created this title to impress my parents of the fact that I was a bit smarter than their border collie. My job as head of the project manager's group was to provide Mr. Frost with a daily dose of gossip on all the project managers. Unfortunately, most of the managers had no life. I had to spend almost an hour reading People magazine to make up stories about the project managers cross linked with Brad Pitt or Britney Spears. Story telling was my forte and I could put a Harvard MBA to shame in that area.

Life was not bad at Fit-Food; we were a group of ignorant and lazy people spreading cheer throughout the obese world. While the Einstein's of the world were without a job we all had jobs for life. The diet food industry was growing at an alarming rate. We had a positive correlation going on with the rate of unemployment, recession, frustration and everything else. We did not have an issue with the FDA either. They never dared taste our food for fear of poisoning. We were not far from the Waste Management facility.

Ever since I was a child, I had made a habit of dreaming things that were achievable within the next twenty four hours. Fit-Food was about to take care of my one long term dream, owning a Waffle House. If Bill Gates were born in the South, he would have the same dream. Just like the dream of every Indian on the planet of owning a Dunkin Donut was turning out to be true, the dream of every person living in the South of owning a Waffle House was going to come true. Life was just beginning to reap rewards.

SHEER LUCK

I am a big fan of the airlines. Not any particular one but all of them. The airlines truly understand the term "customer service" better than anyone else. Imagine dealing with the "shouting voice of the customer (SVOC)" at all times. I have yet to see a single customer behave decently at any airport. I had once read in the in-flight magazine that flight delay was the number one cause of depression in this country. Being Gold or a Platinum member and not being upgraded to First Class was number two. Poor airlines have to deal with the largest number of snobs who feel they are at the top of the world simply due to the accumulation of frequent flier miles.

At Fit-Food all employee airline miles went to Mr. Frost. He personally accompanied each one of us to the airport to collect the miles before we flew.

As I got up from my short nap on the airport floor I realized I still had to reach the gate for my Los Angeles flight. I was texting God as fast as I could not to ruin this one day of the week for me. Friday had to be nice. Struggling through the crowd I finally reached gate D31. "Please hurry," a sweet voice was guiding me, "the plane is about to leave."

It was a different experience holding a First Class ticket in my hand. The airline had been kind to me. For the numerous praise worthy letters that I had written to Customer Service they had sent me over ten guaranteed upgrade certificates. I was shocked. It was like they wanted to honor me as the only person who "cared." I was getting excited at the thought of unlimited free drinks and peanuts without fighting the flight attendant.

"Sir, may I take your coat", the pleasing sound of the flight attendant once again surprised me.

I just wished that someday all the coach seat dwellers would experience the same courteous voice. The text that I had sent to God had been answered. The First Class cabin was wonderful. My Friday was not going to be ruined after all. Instead of shoving my coat underneath the seat I was asked if my coat could be hanged. What could be better?

"Thanks as long as long as you return it at the end of the flight," Memories of college were hard to forget.

It had been a long time since I had sat in the First Class cabin and almost forgot how comfortable it was. The main advantage was that I did not have to occupy half of my neighbor's territory. You also didn't have to walk a mile getting to the bathroom bypassing the forty rows of passengers staring at you like, "Where are you going man?"

The passengers in the First Class cabin all looked fresh and had a glow on their faces. All of a sudden the flight to Los Angeles was not going to be torture after all. I was just hoping that the seat next to me not be occupied by a traveling salesman trying to sell me a time share. I was already in the business of selling snake oil to the world.

Mr. Frost had been in a slump lately. His wife of thirty years had decided to divorce him. She had literally taken a chapter out of *Desperate Housewives* and decided to elope with her thirty year old gardener. Mr. Frost was not worried about her leaving; he was not worried about anyone leaving. He was only worried about the departure of his wealth. The Fit-Food company had only two board members Mr. and Mrs. Frost and now Mr. Frost was worried about the gardener being the third board member.

Besides tackling Mrs. Frost problems, there was another problem brewing up at Fit-Food. One of Mr. Frost's key customer Renaissance Grocers had decided to file for bankruptcy. Renaissance Grocers was one of the bright spots in the food industry growing at a rate of over 30% a year every year. However, they didn't achieve this the old fashioned way. They did not earn it. Renaissance violated every moral, ethics and legal clause applicable to business and humanity.

I still remember the interview Renaissance CEO Herb Maddoff gave after his arrest. "We did nothing different than anyone else, we just got caught, and we were stupid. We should have never printed the pyramid picture in our internal memos." Renaissance filed for bankruptcy.

Mr. Frost was stuck with a big loss from Renaissance. Just like every Renaissance customer we were holding "IOUs" instead of cash and these IOUs were definitely not backed by the United States government. Mr. Frost had advised me to go to each one of the 300 Renaissance stores and pack up our stuff that was not paid for.

At Fit-Food we were also trained in the art of harassing customers who didn't pay on time let alone file for bankruptcy. Unlike most project managers I was a real Black Belt with over a 1000 hours watching UFC.

For all the troubles brewing at Fit-Food I was confident about the success of the company. It had the meanest CEO on the planet and that was good news. I also was optimistic for the simple reason that except for Fit-Food I would not be accepted as a project manager anywhere else on the planet. I was a History major, a complete idiot. This was mediocrity heaven and I loved it.

Mr. Frost was banking on new business with Thomson-Mills, a growing super grocer on the west coast. I knew if we lost this contract, I would be back living with my parents in Minnesota. I was cautiously optimistic knowing well that Mr. Frost always fired someone after a failure of any kind. The only hope was the gardener's position was opening up at Mr. Frost's estate and it did have some perks.

As I was adjusting to my new First Class seat my eyes fell on something I had just placed in the front pocket of the seat—"An idiot's guide to passing the project management certification exam." Mr. Frost had decided that amongst all his project managers the only one who could pass any kind of certification had to be me. His logic was simple. Since, I originated from India I had to be good at math, and if I was good at math I could pass any certification. Going to a training class was out of the question so he had presented me with the guide and warned me to pass or else. It was going to be difficult.

I knew I had enough knowledge about project management to recognize a project from an encounter but not enough to pass any certification exam. Just filling out the application for the certification exam had taken me almost six months. I still remember the sixty days it had taken my project management buddies at Fit-Food to create three different versions of my resume that would add up to 4,000 hours of work experience.

Unfortunately, they had to assume that a week's worth of work was 160 hours instead of 40.

Just as I was about to open my "idiot's guide" I was shocked to see the person occupying the seat next to me. It was Henry Prescott, management consulting guru, the arrogant but highly successful author of at least thirty books on project management. I would not have recognized Henry Prescott in a million years except for his recent pictures everywhere on newspapers and magazine touting him to be next Secretary of Commerce. There is very little that you can't discover about the rich world if you are a People magazine subscriber. Prescott was also a member on the President's council on Business and Finance. The Prescott family was one of the wealthiest in the U.S. amassing immense wealth from their real estate holdings in New York.

I thought by know Prescott should have amassed enough wealth to be on a Gulf Stream but I guess he probably was the black sheep of the family. I couldn't believe my eyes;

I was sitting next to a legend. I wish it was Clint Eastwood but Prescott was alright. I quickly hid my "idiot's guide" before he could realize any special trait in my behavior.

"Hello, I am Henry," the great Prescott introduced himself.

"Balakrishnan Sethurathinam Subramanian," I said, but you can call me B.S.

"Nice meeting you, B.S." He was courteous.

My parents had to be strange. They wanted to give me a unique name that people would not easily forget. They got it right. Not a single person I have ever met has forgotten my name or to make fun of it. Just like my hero "Clint" they now call me B.S. I hated to introduce myself as B.S.; it was awfully close to reality for me. I hated my Indian parents. I wish they were Italian. The only thing Indian parents are known for is the torture of their kids. They made me work eighteen hours on school homework and I was not even out of mother's womb. Since I was an only child I went through hell trying to go through the motions of acting and looking intelligent all through school.

"Please wear your seatbelt, Sir," the courteous voice reminded me of the detriment of flying in an airplane without properly wearing your seat belt. I guess seat belts do save a lot of lives in case of airplane mishaps. It was difficult for me to wear the darn seatbelt without the seat belt extender. Whoever came up with the idea of a seat belt extender had to have a terrific sense of humor aka Borat.

My head was on overdrive. An hour of consulting with Prescott would run upwards of five grand and here he was sitting next to me costing me nothing. I had to take advantage of Henry's knowledge and experience. I had my memory stick ready. I knew if I could extract some of Henry's knowledge on the stick I could easily insert it in my brain.

The funny thing about consultants I had noticed in the past was they become awfully quiet when no money is around. I guess they love to meditate on their free time. I was afraid Henry would enter into a deep state of meditation that could easily last four hours. I could not afford for Henry to meditate.

I was thinking of various ways to get Henry to talk about management, anything about management. I almost thought about introducing myself as the guy from Slumdog Millionaire but I looked too overfed and what if he hated the movie?

It became evident to me that making Henry talk was not going to be easy. It would require begging. Fortunately, humans don't have tails that wag; else it would be really embarrassing.

"So what do you do B.S.," Henry surprised me.

The truth was that most of the time I followed Parkinson's Law—fill time on the job playing solitaire. At Fit-Food no one really knew what they were doing. I was hoping Henry could possibly have some answers to what a project manager at Fit-Food should really be doing besides providing false data on the project. I desperately wanted to hear stories from Henry on how professional project managers saved project.

The last time I had talked with someone of the caliber of Henry was never. It would be interesting to know what a smart person does on a Saturday or Sunday. Do they watch football? Do they even know football? Maybe they watch PBS. They have to be extremely boring. A smart person like Henry can't really discuss anything with anyone as he already knows the answer. It would be a pathetic life to know everything. What would you do?

My hidden agenda was trying to see if Henry could provide me the magic key to pass the certification exam. Ever since they had installed video cameras in the examination center, the percentage of professional project managers coming out from the South had dwindled. On an average the number of certified project managers coming out of the South each year was close to the number of votes Dukakis received on the presidential ballot. He was also very popular in the South.

Life to me was just a reverse Maslow's pyramid. It was slippery at the bottom and easy at the top to walk. In my limited knowledge about understanding the guys who proposed all the motivational theories I also realized that most of them had committed suicide. If Papa Hemingway couldn't stand his own writing who was I to praise his works. The certification exam was taking a toll on my commitment to watching television.

I was hoping for Henry to provide me with an autographed copy of his latest best seller *The Seven Rules of Managing Complexities.* Over the years I had avoided reading anything that started with a seven, but I was hoping Henry's book would change all that. To me humans were born with a single habit and that was not to be habit forming. The seven habits was a made up term by wives who wanted their husbands to be domesticated.

There were some shining stars at Fit-Food. Miguel Alvarez was one of them. Miguel was responsible for maintaining all our machines at Fit-Food. The machines that baked, cooked, and packed all our food. Miguel was good at what he did. He was what we called the equipment whisperer of the South. He would listen to the noise of the equipment and accurately diagnose the problem. His past experience was stealing cars.

Miguel was also a born again philosopher. He sometimes made very thoughtful statements. On many occasions he would remind us that "it is not polite for someone to ask a question to which they know the answer." Henry's question shocked me.

Why would Henry care what I did for a living? It just cost him twenty bucks worth of his time asking me the question.

"Henry, I am a project manager at the Fit-Food Company," I told him.

"That sounds interesting, I am aware of your company and its reputation in the food industry. I bet your job is challenging." He sounded interested in me for whatever reason.

Sure the job was challenging. At Fit-Food any job was challenging. Mr. Frost oversaw every operation. He was the ultimate micro manager demanding to know every detail preferably in the form of color charts. The knowledge of creating charts was as important to the project manager as a Simon to X-Factor. I often thought about the whole profession of project management. Project managers got no respect. They were the most neglected middle managers, hated by customers, disliked by sponsors, back stabbed by team members and beaten up by the buyers. No project manager had ever appeared on Oprah either.

The word "challenging" was a hated word at Fit-Food. We knew when the word "challenging" showed up we had to work evenings, weekends and holidays. Generally, "challenging" to us at Fit-Food was a challenge to understand the mind-set of the customer. At Fit-Food the usual mode of change control was the customer shouting at the top of his voice to make changes midway through the project without paying a dime. It was not unusual to see the customer implementing a change control procedure slapping one of our project managers.

Our Shipping Department was headed by Wendy Belk who used to be Mr. Frost's secretary for twenty years. Her knowledge and experience in the Shipping Department was equivalent to Bernie Maddoff's understanding of ethics and morals as a financial advisor. Wendy had to be a participant on all projects as ex-officio. That was challenging.

Weekend to me was the compromise I had made with God. He gave me hell for the rest of the week and gave me heaven in terms of sports. On weekends I literally could not think anything except beer, food and sports. To me weekend meant only one thing - Football. When they took

Michael Vick to prison I actually went with my savings of $500 to bail him out as I couldn't stand my beloved Atlanta Falcons playing the little leagues and failing. I don't recall missing a football game in twenty years and hope no one I know dies on a weekend to mess it up.

Just then the alarm rang. My time was up for a response to Henry's question.

"Henry, my job is challenging for the simple reason that I am not very good at it," I said honestly.

"B.S., I am a management consultant maybe I can help you if you tell me specifically what you need to know." He sounded so polite I could but only wonder if I was mistaken in my identity of Henry.

There could be other Henry's in the Prescott family and they could all be living in North Dakota and know as much about project management as I would about sunflowers. I had seen the movie *Fargo* ten times and the thought of someone sitting next to me from North Dakota scared the daylights out of me.

Henry definitely had no clue if I knew of him. He was possibly wondering about the entire project management profession looking at my example. But then he should not have been surprised. I had read on one of Google's blogs that 72% of all projects fail and 90% of the project failures are the direct responsibility of the Chinese.

Lately I was getting worried about America's obsession with whining. If it is unemployment we blame the government, if it is swine flu we blame the pigs, if it is our low credit score we blame the rich. At least in the South I have never heard anyone blame the Waffle House for the grease in their arteries. Even the Donald has been blaming the economy for his hair loss.

I was ready for Henry. I was all ears. I was hoping the brain was ready for the tsunami of knowledge it was about to encounter. I was also afraid of the panic it could create within its cerebral territory. Most brains are not evolved to handle excessive information in areas besides sports and gossip. Living in the South, half of my brain's territory was actually a holding place for apple pie and pizzas.

Henry gently took out his reading glasses. He was focused on his mission. Henry, in many ways, looked like Bill Gates. His demeanor, his confidence and his wealth all reminded me of Bill. I had no clue what Bill Gates was all about but I did see him once on television interviewed by Connie Chung. I still remember he got so bored with the interview he just walked off the set and Connie Chung had to settle for being a housewife the rest of her life. Henry could do the same with me. In the middle of our discussions he could just walk off and send me back to my parents as "house kid."

THE LURE

I guess somewhere the opportunity to help others never skips even some of the brightest and the best. Henry sounded extremely enthusiastic to give me advice on project management. I was hoping his advice would be a little more specific to me passing the certification exam. I was cursing the day Mr. Frost found out about the project manager's certification exam. Generally, we were successful at keeping Mr. Frost out of any important details. He was still of the impression that Excel was a University in Berlin. God knows he would never pass the certification exam, but his desire was to have at least somebody in the company call themselves a professional and it had to be me.

I often wondered why one had to pass any kind of certification exam after one already had a college degree. Certification exams were the doing of all those volunteers who needed something to do in their old age. Which human being gets older to volunteer writing exam questions? The whole theory about a good Samaritan is based on cheap labor. Volunteerism to me is another word for cheap. In the South volunteerism meant talking non-stop twenty fours a day.

Human life is blessed with the notion of self-justification at every corner. The first person who started the trend of justification had to be greatest idiot of them all. To me being certified meant you went through the torture and were humiliated. Certification exams I thought were the ultimate nail in the coffin for the South. Everyone knows we were dumb so why rub it in.

When you need help on a project do you look at your certificate or phone a friend? I mean are there cameras in your facilities that block you from calling a friend or opening up a book. The thought of answering questions on a multiple choice exam was scary. The thought of remembering the processes in some form of a country song was even scarier.

Joann King, one of the main buyers for Fit-Food, was my big fan. She wanted to make sure I passed the certification exam and hence had asked the entire town if there was anything specific that could help me pass the certification. The answer came in the form of Rebecca LeMornay, her cousin. Rebecca it seems had attempted the exam about nine times in three years but was getting closer to passing it. Rebecca had the entire processes memorized in the form of a country song. I believe it was "Stand by your Man." I was not sure of all the details but I did know that Rebecca was ugly.

I was actually tempted to tell these stories to Henry. He probably did not have much to do with common people and hence devoid of the comedy of errors. At Fit-Food we were not very different from the actors of faulty towers. The British for all their lack of everything had after all a good sense of humor.

The South was my home and the South loved me. The South loved mediocrity and I was their guy. I was not a red neck, a blue neck or a tattoo neck but they loved me as one of their own. You open that beer bottle with your teeth and you are the South's very own. Larry, the cable guy, could do it and so could Jeff Foxworthy, two of the South's famous children and Nobel laureates.

Where else in the world you experience a cashier at a gas station asking for three forms of I.D. and when you gave him three he would count four and return one.

"B.S.," Henry said in a soft voice. "I can attempt to provide you with some guidance on many general aspects of project management if you provide me with twenty napkins."

I thought Henry had made a mistake listening to me the first time. I was a Fit-Food company project manager not a toilet tissue representative.

"Why you ask for twenty napkins?" I was confused.

"I am going to draw you twenty ideas that would explain the very essence of successful project management," Henry said.

What was I thinking? If Mr. Bezos could create Amazon based upon his idea drawn on one single napkin, I could be in a position to create a whole new IBM with the knowledge on those twenty napkins. I was excited and I just couldn't hide it.

"You got it Henry, I said. I was thrilled as none of the thousands who bought Henry's book had his writing on the napkins. I thought maybe if he initialed each napkin it could be worth more. But at this juncture I did not want to turn him mad.

"B.S., in your opinion what is the single most important factor leading to the success of a project?"

That was a tough question. Studies showed that around 72% of the projects failed; obviously 72% of the project managers had no clue how to lead a successful project. I definitely had no clue as I had never seen a project close at Fit-Food without the customer and Mr. Frost physically going at each other. Sometimes I had to take a punch or two just to defend Mr. Frost. He fought like a woman. I had to be brave in front of Henry.

"Elementary Alex I will take triple constraints for a 1000,"" I had no clue what the answer was but triple constraints sounded technical. In addition Henry did not provide me any choices. Lately, I had been using the word triple constraint a lot. If my customer asked me what the problem was with the delivery I would simply add—"the triple constraints all need to be satisfied—not just yours"

"Hand me napkin #1," Henry said as he pointed towards the twenty napkins I had accumulated.

The Knowledge had begun to flow . . .

The word is Perception

Most of the books I had read on project management in the public library were outdated. The South has more books on the architectural value of waffle houses than project management. The librarian was actually more helpful on answering some of my project questions than the library.

Every project at Fit-Food was a whole new experience. Our organizational process assets consisted of a wooden box containing secret recipes of our diet products, most of them stolen from the competitor's fired workforce. We had no templates we could use. Most of my project managers would think of a template as a hardware tool. It is surprising how modern technology takes so long to reach the South. In the South they have only just begun to enjoy the Karaoke machine.

There was really no chance of referring to any historical information on any of our projects. I had banned our project teams and project managers from performing any lessons learned. Our lessons learned document used to be cruder than Dr. Dre's poetry. In my opinion lessons learned offered nothing more than a reflection of what would definitely happen. In most cases everyone learned lessons naturally at the time of their firing. How do you document things like, "If we had lied to the customer in the first place, we would not face any of the problems we are facing today."

History is filled with incidents where people following past best practices have fallen off the cliff.

I did know a little bit about running projects from my experience as a history major in college. History teaches you that things always repeat themselves. As a History major I also learned that what goes around comes around. I tried to apply these two basic rules to all projects I ran. First, I knew at the beginning of the project that all the bad things that happened on the last project would happen again. This was straight forward. As long as my team remained the same the project results were going to be the same. At Fit-Food you did not have an active directory to choose a team from. It was either Billy or his cousin Joe and they both had the same experience with the law.

Being the greatest country in the world, America sure lacked good project managers. We had good football coaches for sure, good realtors, but no good project managers and no good mayors. Most of the mayors are busy texting their new found love while the city runs out of every needed service. I was getting excited about Henry's approach to project management. Henry lays out his first thought.

Perception 101
Identify 4 corners

I was aware of the triple constraints but where were the four corners. May be if you added the project manager to the triple constraint it became the fourth corner. Maybe Henry's approach was to corner the customer and beat the crap out of him. I did know that the Earth had six corners but then again some might call it continents.

"Henry, I am not familiar with the four corners. Is this a term coined by you?"

"B.S., the four corners of any project are generally considered the four P's—purpose, politics, processes and perception" Henry said, "and yes I will take some credit for coining the term," he added.

I was beginning to see how consultants made their money. While most of us ordinary folks try to improve our vocabulary, trying to move from Southern English to English the consultants are busy coining new terms such as 4-P, 3-G, 5-S, 8-W, P-3, Q-1. The royalty from each one of these terms makes them enough money to send their kids to Ivy League education while ours go to public schools, the only place that reminds us what a Third World country looks like.

It was easy to see how purpose and politics were tied to any project but how does one quantify it or put it in some mode as a variable on any project.

"B.S., I see you are not certain about the four P's, let me explain in simple terms. A project's purpose has to be clearly understood by all stakeholders before the first step of planning begins, the purpose needs to be defined in terms of the product, socio-economic impact and from a greater good to the organization. If there is no real purpose attached to the project as it impacts the betterment of the society or the organization it is a wasted effort."

Henry was right. The whole explanation had to be simple for me. My problem with most books was that I got bored after reading the preface. What I didn't really understand was the fact that if the projects purpose is not well understood by the sponsor or the customer who am I to understand it.

I was thinking the 4-Ps could be my new slogan at Fit-Food. They would instantly love it. Anything that did not involve formulae my team would love it. The whole weight loss industry was running on slogans, we had our own "Be fit, live fit, love fit." I couldn't figure out why our slogan was challenged by the Hard Rock Café people.

Henry's second point was politics. I loved politics. For me there was no difference between politics and gossip. I believed that a gossip that was trusted by peers became politics. If you had enough backers you messed someone up. I thought that was politics. Why was Henry thinking of politics as one of the corners of a project?

At Fit-Food Timmy, Marcus, Jay, Suzy and Denny considered me a seasoned politician. Their definition of a politician was someone who wore clean clothes. They also considered me as the only project manager who had Mr. Frost's ears. Over the years I had made sure their belief was justified.

Mr. Frost had no one's ears. He couldn't even hear without his Wal-Mart hearing device. I did however know the trick to get Mr. Frost listen to me. On occasions I would start pronouncing words in an Indian accent on purpose which got him so mad, he said yes to everything. If you ever heard an Indian person with a Southern accent you would run too.

A Southern and Indian combo statement such as, "As the pan times or false," simply means "Is the project on time or behind schedule."

Einstein could figure out relativity easily but this would send him back to his postal service days.

"B.S., politics play a critical role in most project management organizations. Project priorities can affect the morale of the project team and it is the project manager's responsibility to be pro-active on projects that are deemed to be at the center of upper management's focus. The more you are familiar with the games being played on your project the better risk mitigation strategies you could use."

"Henry, I thought all projects are created equally."

"B.S., all projects are not created equally. In practice projects are treated based on the purpose it serves. Some are simply political projects. Hang on to the projects that will uplift your image and stay away from projects that will put you into retirement earlier." Henry was fairly elaborate on this.

I had figured that in a global economy it was unwise to become a nerd project manager. It was wise of me to have been a History major with Political Science minor to run projects. There is no substitute for political astuteness.

"B.S., politics like risk can also work in your favor if played right. People like Gandhi used politics to turn the masses to think right."

I knew somewhere Gandhi would jump in. You see an Indian and you think Gandhi or more recently a programmer. My parents had hammered in me a lot about the teachings of Gandhi but as a kid I was more interested in the philosophy of Don Henley than Gandhi. If only Henry could explain to me the Gandhian philosophy of project management.

"Henry, do you think there can be anything like the Gandhian philosophy on project management, besides going on hunger strike?" I had to ask.

"Sure, there is. Gandhi was an excellent project manager, his planning was immaculate, he planned over many years. His execution was immaculate including his corrective actions of hunger strike, his team motivation and tracking was phenomenal. He got everyone motivated from poor to rich and his closing was perfect, he achieved independence without bloodshed."

I had this feeling that Henry figured that I wasn't much aware of Gandhi's teachings or philosophy. I always thought Gandhi was a made up character that my parents invented to keep me honest when I was growing up.

The time had come for Henry to help me with my process understanding. Processes were important to me. I needed to memorize quite a few processes to pass my project management certification exam. I honestly didn't want to understand them and I had a bad memory for anything not sports. I was hoping Henry could simplify the entire process puzzle for me in a few words.

"B.S., personally I think processes are overrated. A process is a must but only as a template. The speed at which the technology changes, the approach, tools and techniques constantly need to be updated. Policy guidelines that include a brief description of the processes and their attributes are sufficient for an experienced manager."

I was relieved. Henry was in the same boat as I, albeit I was the mechanic on his million dollar yacht. I thought too there was really no reason to be challenged on processes on the certification exam. Why do I need to memorize processes when the project documents already have process templates? Maybe Henry was pulling my leg. I had read somewhere that all these smart people liked pulling legs of Southerners.

"Henry, I have to agree with you, I hate processes." I was comfortable.

"B.S., you are from the land of Gandhi, you don't hate anyone, may be dislike. Now with respect to processes they are a must for any project but only from an understanding perspective. Once you have gone through several projects, processes should only be used as a reference; it should all be part of continuous improvement."

I finally got it. First, there had to be some logic on why you act a certain way on a project. Next, you had to CYA. The processes provided a long and boring description of why you did what you did, even though what you did really did mess up the project. Third a three ring binder with all kinds of paper filed looks much better than a single paper with coffee spilled all over it.

Processes were definitely a nerd creation. Some people are hell bent on explaining the simplest thing on the planet by writing a book. I was amazed that there were twenty five books written simply on "Learning is a Process." The contents of the book should have been a single word—"Yes."

It finally dawned on me that may be Henry's practical approach makes more sense than the theoretical definition of processes. I could only but smile as I realized the impact of Henry's talk at my kickoff meetings. At Fit-Food a typical kick-off meeting lasted twice as long as the planning process and generally someone got arrested for drunken driving.

"Henry is there any shortcut for me to memorize a whole lot of processes to pass the certification exam?" I had to ask.

"Sure, there is. When I appeared for the certification exam many years ago, I remembered the entire process sequence based on a country song." Henry shocked me

"Well, it had to be the coal miner's daughter," I was on the verification path still shocked.

"No, it was a Hank Williams Sr. song." Henry couldn't control his laughter.

The discussion of country songs brought back some wonderful memories of my time working at the Fit-Food facility in Nashville for about a year. My team members had ensured me that they would make me a fan of country music and country bars. I thought a country bar was a bar in the middle of some farm. Later, I realized that a country bar was simply a place where old folks wore some kind of a fancy hat and square danced. My Nashville stay eventually made me hate country songs with a passion. I had enough of my buddies setting my car radio to 101.5 "we are countreeeee."

The final corner according to Henry was perception. Why would perception play a role in project success? How do you learn to be perceptive? Is there a perception certification I had to pass? I was always keen on becoming perceptive. Maybe perception too can be learned from processes? To percept or not to percept was the question for me.

"Henry, I thought perception was intelligence," I was angling for a specific answer.

"Perception is the ability to understand the culture of your company, the ability to anticipate problems before they occur, understand people issues, very basic really, I am sure you are very perceptive." Henry was encouraging.

"Henry, how do I become more perceptive? Is there a formula for being perceptive?" I wanted more than a general answer from the master.

"Sure, B.S., you can improve your sense of perception. One of the qualities of perception is to be a darn good listener. You have to know how to communicate. The second quality of perception is to look beyond today. Understand the difference between reality and perception. The third quality of perception is reading. Being an avid reader of management journals will allow you to comprehend how successful companies thrive in extremely difficult situations. The more you understand complexities the more you become perceptive."

"Henry is there a simpler way?," I interjected.

"There is, you are born with it. All humans are naturally perceptive. It doesn't matter if it is a project or any other activity you are by nature born perceptive. It is your long built bad habits that prohibit you from using your natural ability."

Henry's words sounded like poetry to me. If all humans are born with it I definitely had a chance. I was in agreement with Henry's philosophy. Bad habits had to be stopped at the Fit-Food company. We generated a bad habit every day. Consultants refused to work with us on fear of forming bad habits working with our project managers which could kill their career.

My parents, both in the medical profession, always talked about perception as a quality that one develops by practicing yoga. Their philosophy was simple. Yoga was the solution to a lot of problems. They used to advise me to practice yoga if I was stuck on a problem. At Fit-Food the project team solved most of their project problems by meditating. Southern meditation also involves eating a lot of fried food.

Learning to Pay Attention

I was overloaded with the knowledge from Henry's first napkin. I was afraid it was going to be lot more information than I had anticipated. I had an uncanny ability to fall asleep in the middle of meetings, even meetings where I was the moderator. However, Henry's sermons had me wide awake and alert. The First Class seat was a big help too. The drinks were flowing and there were no fights for the additional peanuts.

"Pass me the second napkin." Henry was bent on teaching me project management.

My mind was all over. I was thinking of selling these napkins on E-Bay. This had to be my lucky break. I was being taught by the whiz of management, the man who was quoted more on management then Buffett on Stock Market. A selfless man was helping his fellow passenger, strike it rich on E-Bay. This had to be America.

"Henry, please accept the second napkin." I felt like a kid on his first day of school. Let the learning begin.

This time it looked as if Henry was writing more than one word. It was an encouraging sign.

"Here, B.S., see if it makes sense to you." Henry's writing once again was immaculate.

A Project and A Project Manager are inseparable

The advantage of being someone like Henry Prescott is the fact that no matter what you say people believe there has to be a deeper meaning. I knew there had to be something more to "a project and a project manager are inseparable." At Fit-Food if the project sank, you as a project manager sank with it. If the project succeeded you definitely violated SOX or GAAP regulations.

Why would Henry put a simple thought on the napkin? My days of selling on E-Bay looked numbered. Inquiring minds needed to know more. I had to ask the question.

"Henry it sounds simple, is there a deeper implication to this sentence."

"B.S., the project charter only confirms the validity and feasibility of an idea. The project manager is responsible for creation of the product. There is a difference between reality and perception at every stage of the project. The more fully you understand the project manager the more fully you understand the project and vice versa. The project manager is the trust factor behind the recognition of the product as something useful."

"I thought the product is what the customer wants, the project manager was useless to him. That's how it works at Fit-Food Henry."

"B.S., you are underestimating the field of project management. Billions of dollars are lost because of the lack of support and respect provided to project managers. The project manager in essence is the driver of the project. Unless the project manager is completely committed to the project and is loyal to the project the project will not work. The perspective of the project manager in handling the project is the single most important factor in the project's success."

"Henry, can you put it in 1, 2, 3 . . .form, the folks at Fit-Food will have a difficult time with entire paragraphs."

"O.K. let me put it in the 1, 2, 3,.format for you." Henry was comfortable even with me irritating the heck out of him.

"1 A project manager works solely for the success of a project.

2 A project manager can use any means to achieve project success as long as it is ethical.

3 A project success is solely attributed to the competency of the project manager.

4 A brilliant project manager does not exist, only a pragmatic one.

5 All successful projects are tied by a single common thread—the project manager.

6 The gold standard in project management changes constantly."

Henry had done it for me. I could use these points to establish my power further at Fit-Food. For all my drawbacks as an intellectual I was exceptional at power point. In fact in the entire South if you know power point you are a qualified project manager. I could envision the format for the six points in my head. Life could be good.

I finally began to see the wisdom of the statement Henry had made. Project managers did not always believe in their projects. If a project is treated as a task it is not good enough. At Fit-Food every project was a step towards revenge aimed at Mr. Frost. With the salaries frozen over 10 years, all projects had to thaw before they ran.

"B.S., as a project manager I am sure you trust your instincts on all projects."

I was really not sure if I was loyal to projects. At Fit-Food most projects were about coming up with new products for the overweight population. It was difficult at times to understand how coming up with a new product that took less baking time would help dieters. I guess research showed that the food deprived population can't even wait five minutes before the food is prepared in the microwave;

they put their mouth in the microwave and burn it. How were my projects helping the community?

"Henry, do you have to love the projects you are managing? Can you not dislike what you are doing and still be good?"

"B.S., frustration beyond a certain level is not healthy. At the end of the day a project manager can't be separated from the project. You will become the project. Your life will begin to imitate the project."

Henry's fundamental understanding of the project impressed me. He could relate to the project as if he was talking about his best friend.

I was hoping that Henry's next thought would be something that could help me with the certification exam. A little inside information from his connections at the Institute would surely help.

BACK TO PROCESS . . .

The flight to Los Angeles couldn't have been better. The gourmet dinner served on china was a marked difference from the twenty five cents peanuts imported from Georgia's contaminated plants. I was dining with one of the smartest men on the planet and if not for anything else just by way of osmosis some knowledge was bound to flow my way.

There were several hours left for the flight to reach Los Angeles and I was not about to let Henry take a breather. Suddenly I noticed Henry was looking at his watch. The geniuses have a trait of doing exactly what they feel like. If Henry felt it was time to sleep I knew it would be the end of life for the remaining eighteen napkins.

I was not the one to let go of things that easily, gently I made sure the third napkin had been placed appropriately.

"Thanks, B.S. I appreciate your paying attention."

Henry scribbled one more time. His writing, once again immaculate. The person who was giving advice to the President's council on business and industry was all set to impart his knowledge to a project manager from Fit-Food, a company solely surviving on the mere weakness of human beings fascination for food.

As I watched Henry scribble on the napkin, I noticed he had not once looked at his blackberry or his IPhone. That was a clear indication he had "arrived." I could not fathom anyone smart being addicted to a blackberry. Henry had self-control. Living in the South I really had no need for a blackberry. In the South the wireless towers didn't transmit data, only voice. Data serves no propose if no one can read it.

The process equation was not completely out of Henry's mind as evidenced by his next thought.

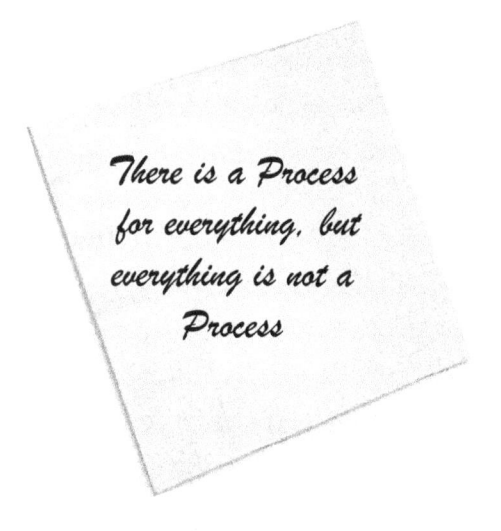

There is a Process for everything, but everything is not a Process

The writing on the third napkin surprised me.

I had always believed that following a process for everything was a big waste of time. With me it was gut reaction most of the time and I figured it was the same with all my comrades Timmy, Marcus, Jay and Suzy. However, the statement coming from Henry was surprising.

"B.S., let's revisit the area of processes for a second. When I said follow the processes as a guideline I meant that a process can't function in real time as human instinct. There are rules within the bounds of a project and there are instances where processes do little to help you."

I realized Henry was not making much sense. He lost me with "rules within the bound of any project." I thought projects had no rules. You bend the rules and cook the rules in order for projects to be successful. Sometimes you have to make rules that counteract the rules that give you trouble. I had made up so many rules of my own that sometimes I couldn't even follow my own rules even though they were all designed to save me.

My sense was Henry sometimes felt he was talking to an IBM executive and had to be politically correct. I decided to understand Henry's approach by using the smoothing technique I was so used to at Fit-Food.

"Henry, are we saying when your house is on fire, you run out the door, there is no need to refer to the process book stored in the kitchen drawer."

"Not quite, but you got it. The human instinct processes several bits of information that is based on a pre-defined process, continuous improvement strategies, feedback and corrective actions all at once. It is prudent to differentiate routine situations on a project versus extraordinary."

There were several extra ordinary situations we had to go through with each of our projects. In most cases these involved finding the people who were supposed to finish their assigned tasks. Most of the team members who were not on the critical path took long vacations simply on the basis of knowing there were floats on the project. The union laws didn't allow us to put anyone to work on the critical path if they were on the float. This was one of the key reasons why most of our project boats sank.

Henry I thought was trying to imply that there has to be a reflex action to many of the things you do as a project manager.

"Henry, are we talking reflex actions?"

I had to clarify before I wandered off in the wrong direction, which in my case would not take more than an instant.

"B.S. you nailed it. Reflexes are developed as a matter of practical learning experience applied to critical situations; these are knowledge centers which bypass a whole lot of documents and processes."

"I get it. So plan in accordance with a theme but execute in accordance with gut." I surprised myself.

"B.S., I got to write that on a napkin and start my own B.S. collection." He was smiling.

I figured Henry was revealing more than I understood on all these napkins. I was happy that Henry considered himself a project manager in spite of the executive kind of things he did. I always felt we needed solid project managers who would raise the image of project managers universally. In my opinion the whole field of project management did not get the respect it deserved. It was like if you are "alive" you can run projects.

I liked the thought of reflex actions. The only reflex actions I was aware of were reflex actions granted to humans by God, at least until the age of fifty, which ensured that when certain crisis occurred humans did not take an eternity to react. I used to lecture my protégé Denny many times on reflex actions. "If your hand accidentally gets into a flame you don't ask your boss what to do, you pull it out."

"Henry, I like your approach to solving problems. You have a direct way of saying things. You don't talk in technical terms but plain simple English." I had to shower some praise on the individual who was inserting power chips in my brain.

"B.S., I am not saying anything unique, the proven way to running successful projects is to differentiate facts from anecdotes, information from data, efficiency from waste and experience from books."

The third napkin had taught me an important lesson. There was plenty of room for me to improve in my existing job. I had the ability to take Fit-Food where not many weight loss companies had gone before—"out of bankruptcy."

Quietly I handed Henry the fourth napkin as the hostess refilled my beer and his mineral water.

"Sir, do you want anything else."

"Please pack me a bag of peanuts to go." I couldn't resist the temptation.

Baselines are Only a Guideline

Henry was comfortable in the teacher's role. I realized his focus had shifted from just delivering the sermon to making sure I understood. I was impressed by Henry's teaching style. His mastery of the subject matter was equally balanced by his simplicity of explanation. I wish my college professors had his ability to teach. Thanks to being tenured, they didn't have to.

The fourth napkin had made its way towards Henry's Mont Blanc. I was curious if the Mont Blanc was making his righting so meticulous. I was hoping Henry would initial all the napkins; however I was too timid to ask him.

"Henry, can you put your initials on all these napkins. I just want to keep them separate from all the other napkins I have used to clear the beer spill."

"No problem B.S., I will put my initials on all these napkins."

I was hoping E-Bay would not declare bankruptcy before I landed in LA. There was a possibility with its latest round of earnings results. I was feeling guilty taking advantage of Henry's time but with me guilt lasted only a few seconds. My parents had taught me the cure, all I had to do was say

"OM" and I was cured of feeling any guilt. A major guilt took a more serious approach—a dip in the Ganges River. With my work at Fit-Food I was on a weekly shuttle to the Ganges along with all the Wall Street advisors and the Maddoff family.

The fourth napkin addressed the subject of baseline.

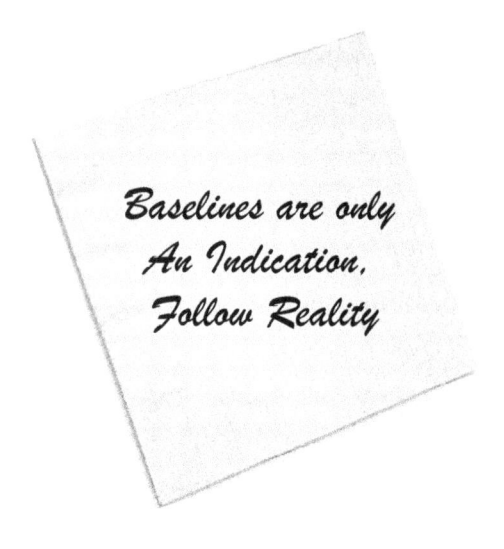

Baselines are only
An Indication.
Follow Reality

"B.S., performance measurement baselines are important to a project but baselines can't be blindly followed."

I had a tough time with baselines. I always knew that baselines were the creation of project managers. However, at Fit-Food, Mr. Frost had to sign on each of the baselines whether he understood the project or not. As the leader of the project manager's group I had the misfortune of signing along with him on all the baselines.

Generally, we had three baselines to begin with for each one of our projects. One was pessimistic, one was overly pessimistic and one was reality which was truly pessimistic.

Henry once again surprised me. Was Henry implying baselines are "informal?" I thought before I opened my mouth, I needed to think this through. I looked out of the window and all I could see were dark clouds. That was not the sign I was looking for. I acted as if I was in deep thought.

"There B.S. where have you gone? "Henry asked looking puzzled.

"I have been thinking Henry on this one and I believe you are going against traditional wisdom on this one."

I was up for a challenge but only slightly.

I didn't even know what traditional wisdom meant. To me traditional wisdom was a speech given by someone who had just lost the election. Traditional wisdom sometimes also meant that the person was dead. I was hoping I could take back my statement but if I did that repeatedly I would cease to exist.

"Henry I thought baselines were the real truth, if you missed them you were in trouble."

"Well O.K. but baselines are created at a certain point in time, and that point in time is long gone when the project is being executed.

Baselines simply serve as an indicator of the expectations of management and in some cases limitations. It is the responsibility of the project manager to sync perception with reality by providing facts as the project progresses."

"Henry, but aren't you constrained by the baseline, the baselines are set as a reflection of the project objectives." Someone inside me was speaking and I had no clue.

"You make a good point B.S., the baselines are set to objectives, but objectives of a project can be achieved several different ways, the objectives itself are a function of time."

I liked Henry's terminology, "function of time." To me the word function of anything made for an impressive conversation. At Fit-Food one of the surest ways to confuse Mr. Frost was to use the words function and derivative in the same sentence. It was like giving a Southerner a statistical calculator with more than five keys.

"B.S., all I am saying is that a baseline is a guidance and you can't get too rigid with that concept or else your natural optimizing ability to work on projects disappear."

"Henry, at Fit-Food we have to magically stick to the numbers assigned by Mr. Frost. The only alternative for us if we mess up is to set one of the conveyor lines on fire. That generally confuses the heck out of everyone. In general we use *force majeure* about twice on a project. Even Mr. Frost is scared of *force majeure.*"

"B.S., try to negotiate with your boss, explain to him the difference between forecasts and dynamic demands, explain to him the time value of knowledge and expectations of returns on objectives. Ask him if he thinks the objectives of the project are tied to time?"

Henry was scaring me. It was one thing to miss the baseline, it was completely a different animal to discuss with your boss that baselines really are only a guideline. It would be O.K. if you had another job lined up, but for the many at Fit-Food that was not an alternative. The Waffle House could support only so many employees.

The thing I learned from Henry was to fight over every baseline we created with Mr. Frost. If only the definition of baseline would change we would be O.K. Whoever came up with the definition of "a baseline as an approved estimate" never met the guy who approved it. The tenured academicians probably are of the belief that baselines are approved after everyone jointly sang "we are the world."

Over the past five years my parents had send me numerous books on management and leadership. Some of these books however belonged to the management of healthcare; they probably got them free from the salespeople who constantly bribe the doctors with gifts. Honestly all these books had given me a headache. I even tried to subscribe to the Harvard Business Review but they had stopped subscription to anyone with an IQ below 75.

In all the excitement of Henry teaching me I had forgotten all about Mr. Frost. I suddenly became aware that all the knowledge I was inheriting from Henry was surely going to put me out of job.

"Henry, have you heard the term manage by decade."

"No, B.S., I guess I missed that."

"Well, Mr. Frost's management style is to "manage by decade." In this decade he has decided that since the supply of project managers far exceeds the demand, he can set the baseline to whatever he wants. Our work week at Fit-Food is generally around 70 hours without counting the weekend."

"I am sure there is a law against it," Henry added.

Sure there was a law against it, but Henry had not met our Human Resources Manager, Judy Watson. She was accused of sexual harassment by every male employee at Fit-Food including the ugliest member of the Fit-Food family Tom Pickens. Judy was Mr. Frost's niece and fully loaded at 400 pounds. I was thinking there are laws and there are laws and then there is Judy.

For a diet food producer we had the highest percentage of 400 lb. people. Our Scatter diagram of age versus weight was so positively correlated it exploded in the end.

Motivation does not need a Reason

It was time for the fifth napkin to take its rightful place in front of the great master. An ordinary napkin will hold extraordinary value in a few minutes.

"Henry, be careful my brain has a limited capacity and probably lacks a graphics processor. I can only understand plain simple terms," I said, confident in my joking with Henry.

I knew somewhere along the way the term team would appear. I was afraid of that. The mere mention of team members scared me. At Fit-Food we were in a perennial storming mode. There was no need for forming as everyone was related. The thought of putting Kimberly, Sam, Greg and Rose on another project would scare the daylights out of any human being.

Kimberly had to be on every project as a scheduler. She knew Excel and was qualified. Sam was good at drawing sketches and hence was a natural fit for any graphical activity. Greg was our quality guy. If there was any reason for the swine flu to hit the South it had to be Greg. There was an awful lot of stuff Greg knew but none of that was legal or related to quality. Rose was generally put on projects to follow Greg before the Sheriff got him. The rest of the team considered these four as their Ocean's Eleven partners.

Henry's next thought was about teams. Henry probably had similar experience with teams as I. His thoughts bordered on the pessimistic side. I always thought motivation was over rated. It was once again coined by philosophers over a bar brawl. I really believed that Maslow got the pyramid all wrong. The pyramid should be upside down, you would then be able to clearly see people throwing people down the pyramid.

"B.S., this is something I am sure you are a master of." Henry was perceptive.

Team Motivation Changes Daily, PM's Motivation Needs to be Consistent

I had to admit this was a little easier for me to understand than all the other napkins combined. My belief was simple—a human being from the South could not be motivated by another human being from the South. In the South human beings got motivated for revenge. On every project I had to introduce the term revenge in some manner to get the team motivated. Jealousy was another factor they loved.

My teams were fond of the late night infomercials on motivation as they provided simple facts for getting motivated—walk, exercise, turn on the light, meditate, don't kill yourself. In the South infomercials hold a better Nielsen ranking than Letterman.

"Henry, I got it. People suck. I agree. I have always believed that team motivation was overrated. A motivated team is a team that masters the art of backstabbing the project manager." I was so excited I just couldn't hide it.

"B.S., I didn't mean to bring up your softer side but what I was referring to is the manager's focus has to be constant throughout the project irrespective of the setbacks, whereas the team can always take a breather. The responsibilities are different and so is the objective." Henry looked serious.

"An effective team is one where the main focus of each team member is to accomplish their own task satisfactorily and only worry about interactions where need be. The more focused they are on their own work the easy the interaction. The project manager's perspective is the opposite. It is entirely on the integration aspect. It is solely focused on the inter connections of the teams."

"Group dynamics and individual dynamics are also different. In running successful projects, the project manager needs to emphasize to the group "how" team dynamics impacts the success of the project," Henry added.

There was no team dynamics at Fit-Food. To me team dynamics meant understanding the whole was better than the sum of its parts. At Fit-Food the team did not understand the whole or the parts. Consultants had requested me to stop team exercises. One of the exercises we had tried before was to let a team member fall backwards and to let someone hold him. That did not work. Denny still suffers from memory lapses sometimes.

Unfortunately, his memory lapses always result in his forgetting how to perform the tasks.

I looked at my watch and was relieved that there was sufficient time for Henry to complete all the napkin art. The flow of free snacks was also keeping my brain cells charged up. It seemed as if the flight attendants in the First Class cabin had actually attended a customer service class. The flight attendants in the coach looked like they came straight from the North Korean camps. I was even afraid to look back at the coach section.

Henry's flow of knowledge was bringing me closer to understanding Newton's theory of relativity, or was it Einstein's theory? I was now able to understand the role of the falling apple leading to Newton's discovery. I was going to make sure we had plenty of them apples at Fit-Food.

"B.S., I am sure you have read the autobiography of Mahatma Gandhi—My Experiments with Truth, it is a true depiction of the power of human motivation."

"Henry, I am afraid of experimenting with truth, but I will definitely read it. My parents had read me so many stories when I was a kid that all these stories have kind of got mixed up in my brain. I still get confused between Gandhi and Ben Kingsley."

Henry probably was looking for the door to jump but at 35,000 feet even his ego could not keep him afloat.

Managing a Rural Team

Pick me; pick me, Napkin number six identified itself. I had hoped that Henry would not lose interest in the middle of all this and just tell me that he had enough preaching but Henry showed no signs of boredom.

The smooth airplane ride was making a difference in my thinking. I was getting excited at the thought of Mr. Frost firing me someday. I could start with a company that practices some of the things Henry was saying. I realized my parents were right all along in preaching the value of knowledge except they did in a very boring manner, which kind of killed my motivation.

"B.S. have you seen the Godfather?"

The question startled me. The Godfather was one of my favorite movies. I loved the violence. Maybe Henry liked the violence. Was he telling me to take care of the team the Godfather way? As far as I knew none of the team members owned a horse. I was afraid he was trying to tell me he had become my Godfather and I had to touch his hand or something. I was perplexed, why would he ask me if I had seen the Godfather?

"Only about seven times," I replied in the same tone as Marlon.

"Well then you should be able to easily see why I put the next thought down,"

I ordered Napkin number six to take its place in front of the Godfather.

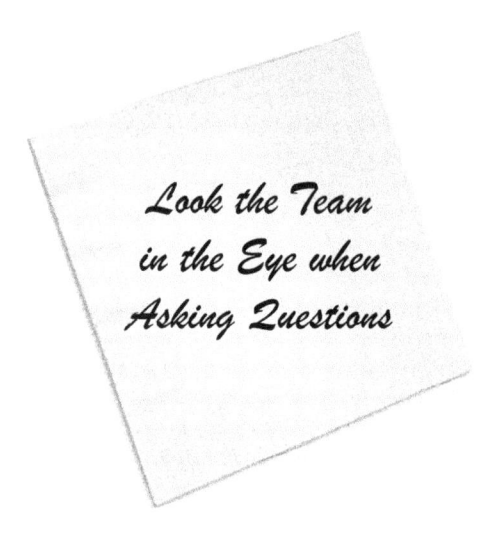

Look the Team in the Eye when Asking Questions

Looking the team in the eye also involved looking at their faces, a sight not so pretty. The South was noted for ugly employees. Why would it be a big deal to look anyone straight in the eye?

I generally looked at their shoes when I asked questions and believe me there were no Jimmy Choo or even Johnston and Murphy hiding there.

I did understand what Henry was trying to preach and that was "straight talk." The statement looked more like an infomercial motivational statement, something the rich man's guru Tony Robbins would say.

"Henry, I can see the advantage of looking into the eye and asking questions but why do you regard this as a big deal."

"It is a big deal. Without realization of truth and honesty you are going nowhere on the project. Remember project management is a team sport, a team that trusts each other is a good team but a team that is honest with the project manager wins"

I had seen somewhere in my dummy's guide about communication. The dummy had written that most of the communication was non-verbal. I would love to shut the teams' mouth with superglue and let them communicate effectively on a project non verbally for about a month.

"Henry, are you talking about all the fancy ways to communicate, it doesn't work at Fit-Food."

"B.S., I am simply referring to the fact that there is no substitute for honesty on projects. The best way to trust someone is to make a habit of looking straight in their eyes and talking."

"Does that really work?"

"Yes it does. I have been looking at your eyes and I can tell you are an extremely honest person."

I couldn't be honest if God hit me on the head. Through my eyes Henry possibly could see my silky smooth Cerebrum. Geniuses are generally very good at reading people but in my case Henry's reputation was at stake.

"B.S. let me tell you a secret." Henry was done explaining napkin number six. "Every time you look someone in the eyes and ask questions they are afraid you are reading them carefully and would hesitate to wander off too much in the wrong direction. The more direct your stare the more fear they have lying to you." Henry sounded like Inspector Cousteau.

I was comparing my time with Henry to my sixty year old boss who started every sentence with, "You don't have a clue, do you?" My colleagues at Fit-Food had asked me to start an association for the rehab of all stressed out project managers where we could all meditate and then curse out Mr. Frost with acronyms. Suddenly, it hit upon me. I could invite Henry to talk at our local semi-professional project management group meeting.

"Henry, I would love to have you talk at our semi-professional project management chapter meetings, currently, we have no interesting speakers except for salespeople who try to sell everything from calculators to dummy books for idiots. The local chapter has almost become a pizza and beer joint for desperate project managers," I told him offering him the deal of a lifetime.

"I will try to make it to one of your meetings," Henry said politely.

I knew he was bluffing as he did not look me straight in the eye but looked at my shoes—non-polished and cheap. He probably couldn't stop his laughter.

SUCCESS IS NOT SO SUCCESSFUL

Project management is definitely a strange field. No one has been able to clearly define the role of the project manager. Somewhere there is a whole lot of talk about the qualities a project manager has to possess. This to me is ridiculous. It seems that a project manager has to be a negotiator, a leader, a coordinator, a manager, a motivational guru and a communicator. Are you going to get all that in a person at minimum wage?

The field of project management is the only field that differentiates a project manager from a professional project manager who by the way has passed some kind of a multiple choice exam. Do we have doctors versus professional doctors? Lawyers versus professional lawyers? Dentists versus professional dentists? How would you categorize a non-professional project manager? It could be, "I am not a real project manager, but I did stay at the Holiday Inn last night?"

I was equally confused by the statistical data that professionals in the project management field were putting out. Surveys always showed that "most projects failed." If most projects failed why even do anything. Is there anyone who really wants to start something that always fails? Who in the world would want to build a boat and see it sink?

I noticed that Henry's focus was more on approach and environment rather than strict theories. He was keen on integration of the existing environment with the boundaries of the project. No wonder Henry was well rewarded. I wanted to hire Henry as a consultant for Fit-Food but knew the odds. In general we had to threaten the consultants to work at Fit-Food by keeping their families hostage.

Henry's strategy for success was not a whole bunch of formulae, it was a practical approach combining patience, perseverance, ethics and loyalty all factors that I severely lacked.

"B.S., here is my thought on how projects can be successful, you don't underestimate the success, you overestimate."

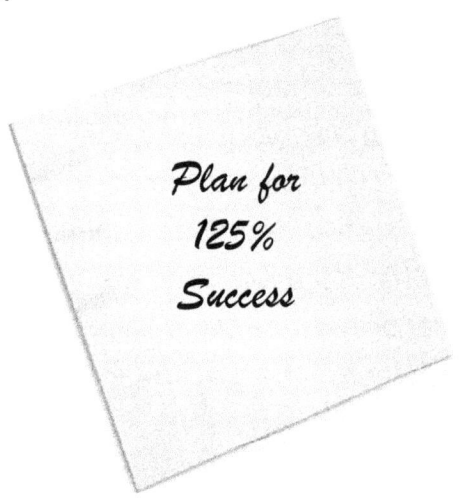

Planning for 125% success sounded like a cliché. I wouldn't know cliché if it sang to me, however as a spelling bee contestant I had to spell cliché once. I know I didn't make my parents happy that day or for that matter any day since then.

"Henry, why would I contemplate 125% success when achieving 50% success was impossible?"

"B.S., you don't shoot for 50% success do you?"

By the time the project began I was generally so frustrated that I didn't know what I was shooting for. To me every project had a beginning but no end in sight. Our customers dictated the product they wanted to see on their shelf. Mr. Frost wanted to see money in the bank. The research staff wanted protection against their infringing on the competitor's formulae.

"Henry, as a project manager I shoot for 100% success on all my projects, as a human being I shoot for forgiveness and as a Southerner I shoot for fried chicken."

"B.S., I thought you would be a vegetarian. I am a vegetarian by choice for the past thirty years. I thought people from Southern India were mostly vegetarians."

"Sure Henry, people from Southern India are all vegetarians, but people here in the deep South live on fried chicken. They made me taste a religious chicken they called it Church's Chicken and ever since that day I lost my vegetarianism."

"B.S., let's focus on the 125% success formulae. Just as you focus on statistics related to failure of projects you should also focus on opportunities available for any project to super succeed."

Henry probably was using the consulting lingo. The kind of stuff Wall Street CEOs love to tell their shareholders just before their indictment. It was difficult for me to gold plate the success number. I had enough trouble manipulating the failure numbers as it was.

"Henry, are you telling me there has to be a process called planning for 125% success?"

"Yes my Indian friend. There has to be a process that lays out completely the thoughts and process of achieving a higher success rate than 100%."

I realized I no longer was a passenger on the plane. I was Henry's friend. I could introduce myself at all the professional seminars as Henry's friend. I could call the President of the United States and say I was Henry's friend. I could use the "referent" power to my full advantage. I knew I had forgotten to take my pills.

I was never a big believer in planning. I always thought planning was simply done to protect you from frivolous lawsuits. Planning for success was a good idea for me as I was a constant observer to planning for failure at the Fit-Food company.

At Fit-Food it was not uncommon for project managers to steal documents from each other in order to complete a project management plan. It was also not uncommon to discover activities on a project that belonged to a completely different project from the past that had no relevance to the current project.

I had to discipline myself. My overindulgence with my own life as a project manager was not helping me digest Henry's message clearly.

Henry probably realized my uneasiness and immediately took action to make me comfortable.

"B.S., project management unlike any other field is very closely tied to the environment. The best you can do as a project manager is to "live" the project. Enjoy the experience."

Henry's point was straightforward. I realized that most of the people at work today didn't seem happy, ate alone during lunch and skipped the office parties. People had lost that "touchy" feeling.

Henry was eager to take me to the success strategy.

"Planning for 125% success comes from the simple fact that just as uncertainty leads to problems it can equally lead to opportunities. Projects need to be analyzed from the perspective of constant improvements. The human psychology always anticipates problems when it should constantly anticipate opportunities. Think about completing a college degree in three years instead of six years," Henry was in a justification mode.

Henry unfortunately had hit upon a sore subject for me. The mere mention of college brought tears to my eyes. I believed colleges in the United States were headed towards two simple categories: party school and suspended party schools. Colleges were the last frontier of pseudo intellectuals who were also tenured who had not stepped out of the confines of the college campus to face reality.

My History professors were at least honest. They told me that the History majors had no future and that we should be thinking about other careers after graduation. The best a History major could do would become a manager of produce at Kroger. They generally required you to know the history of where the products came from.

I was reminded of Robert Palmer's song, some majors have all the fun and some majors have none at all. Believe me, a History major had nothing but fun, but now it was hurting.

I was still confused with Henry's 125% solution.

"Henry, I still don't get the 125%."

"B.S., the thought of achieving or targeting 125% success stems from the simple fact that just as we consider failure of projects as a norm, in the future we need to develop a culture where achieving 125% success becomes the norm, does it makes sense?"

"No."

"O.K., suppose you are applying for a job, does your resume reflect 100% of your ability or 125% of your ability."

I knew what the answer to that question was. My resume was based on the simple fact that no company had the time to check all the details on the resume. At Fit-Food we knew not to look at resumes of people when assigning tasks to team members.

"Henry, I am beginning to finally understand."

"Our attitude with projects needs to change, we are now extremely comfortable with the concept and applications of six sigma philosophies but project management is still considered completely subjective, you can really achieve 125% success on every project." Henry once again got passionate.

Henry did not have to be this longwinded. All he had to tell me was "trust me." He had me at "Hello."

Henry was truly an intellectual. He enjoyed every word he said and he said it with passion. I wish my successful parents had taught me the lesson of life with a decent English accent and a smile. I could have been the pride of India. I could have been an extra in the Slumdog movie.

THE "WHY BOTHER?" GENERATION

I did know a little bit more about Henry from the newspaper articles. He had the reputation of being ruthless when it came to cost reduction. He was singularly responsible for the unemployment rise from 9% to 10% in this country. Henry had quickly risen through the exclusive leadership club by his sheer ability to negotiate.

Henry was one of the youngest to have been credited with creation of a three tiered "system-project-portfolio pyramid" the de facto standard for most organizations running portfolio simulations. I personally had not the faintest clue as to what it meant or what it did except for the fact that the man who created it was the one teaching me project 101.

I thought for a moment about my own ability to teach. Lately, I was assigned to teach Suzanne, Randy and Robert the new hires at Fit-Food about project management. I still can't forget those sessions where Suzanne would nag me saying, "There has to be more than that to understand the field of project management." I wish I had the napkins, in the least I would have been able to impress Suzanne.

Randy and Robert belonged to the same class as the rest of us where less was better and nothing was the best.

I had these urges all of a sudden to learn new things. Lady luck could be shining on me. On my return flight from Los Angeles the person sitting next to me could be the moderator for the professional certification exam. He could tell me all the stupid ways they frame exam questions. He could tell me all the silly secrets of interpreting the questions. That would put an end to all the naysayers at Fit-Food who believed that the chances of my passing the certification exam were less than China declaring democracy. The two hundred napkins could hold the two hundred questions on the exam.

Day dreaming was second nature to all of us working at Fit-Food. Standing next to diet food all day could force even his holiness the Dalai Lama to day dream.

Henry was ready with the eight thought. It was once again a non-complicated statement, in plain simple English and few words, just the way I liked it.

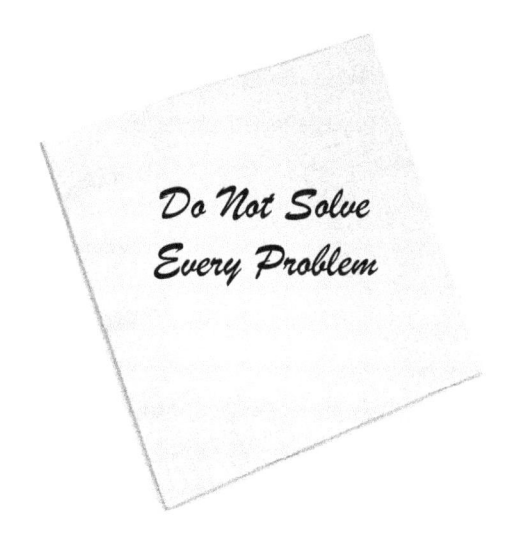

*Do Not Solve
Every Problem*

This was easy for me to understand. I wish Henry had more napkins like this. I never tried to solve every problem albeit I couldn't recognize every problem if hit me in the head. I was confident Henry was implying that solving every problem would be contemplated as "gold plating" but Henry had a different answer.

"There is never a matter of optimality on every project, only near optimality and as long as you are within the bounds of optimality you have achieved your goals."

I was thinking about using this fancy word "optimality" at our next project manager's meeting. This was sure going to impress all the project managers. It would almost be like Dennis Miller broadcasting the football games. In many ways the project managers at Fit-Food looked up to me for new ideas. They were an extremely patient bunch as most of the time the wait was significantly long for ideas to show up.

"Henry, the word optimality, is this a mathematical equation?"

"You are teasing me."

No I wasn't, but the answer was "Yes."

The concept of "do not solve every problem" seemed coming from someone who could be on the Oprah Show. I could imagine someone making a statement "do not solve every problem" and tears flowing from the audience..."he is so right."

One of the policies at Fit-Food was the television' had to be on all the time. For some strange reason Mr. Frost believed that most managers got their ideas for work improvement from television. Everyone in the workplace was a TV addict. I don't know if anyone really got any ideas from a picture tube but I sure could predict the outcome on *"Days of our Lives."* In the South watching soaps for men is a politically right thing to do.

"Henry, I don't understand. Are you talking about knowing a problem and ignoring it based on its significance or randomly throwing away a certain percentage of problems, kind of pre-test problems on some of the certification exam." I had to bring in the word certification one way or the other.

"B.S., do not solve every problem simply relates to the responsibility that the project manager has towards fulfilling the objective. It is easy to get carried away with the intention of planning for pro-activeness to the point where you miss the forest looking at trees. The comprehension of major objectives should be clearly differentiated with specific issues and problems."

"Henry, I get your point. Sometimes the urge to solve every little problem can make the project manager lose his focus on the key objectives."

"B.S., are you repeating what I just said." Henry was smiling.

I was wondering if I was violating some kind of copyright law by repeating Henry's exact word. I was going to use a pseudonym for Henry to quote everything he had told me. The pseudonym was going to be my name.

"Henry, how do you approach a problem," I finally asked. It was a tough question.

"You look at a problem, remove all emotion in evaluating it and resolve it always in favor of the project."

Henry did look a little bit like Jack; maybe Jack had stolen his dialogue. I also noticed that Henry never raised his voice. He was extremely soft spoken something I was not used to at Fit-Food. At Fit-Food the soft spoken people were counted as having some kind of a disorder. They were constantly harassed. "Don't you eat enough to speak up clearly," Aunt Emily would shout.

"Henry, in your opinion is it better to be a decision maker or a thinker."

"B.S., a good decision maker relies on good information. Good information comes from a lot of sources. Trust is key to good decisions and so is data integrity. So to answer your question it is not a matter of speed but approach. What is important however is that, once you have the information to make the decision there should be no delay.

Over analyzing a problem is the worst form of decision making."

"Over analyzing is not an issue at Fit-Food, we are talking mass under analyzing. At Fit-Food we take a problem, put emotion in it, always look at what's in it for me, and resolve it to mess up everyone's schedule. The owner loves it."

"It can't be that bad at Fit-Food. You are in the business of making people happy," Henry was trying to resist laughter.

I never thought of Fit-Food as a happiness generating company. May be Henry was mistaken about Fit-Food being Fast-Food.

At Fit-Food we were asked to be kind to the fast food companies. They were the reason our business was booming. We all were given significant amount of coupons to eat at all the fast food joints. All the eating at Fast-Food had taken a toll on my body. I no longer could be mistaken for Brad, Pitt that is.

Henry was correct however. I had recently observed an incident which made sense of Henry's interpretation of Fit-Food as a happiness generating company. On a recent flight to Denver, the airline had run out of seat belt extenders and was planning to tie down all the fat passengers with some kind of a rope in the name of safety regulation. That was one of the most embarrassing situations in my life.

"B.S., remember do not be a micro-manager. A project manager solves only problems that are essential to achieving the projects objectives."

"Aye aye, captain," Sulu out.

I was still deeply absorbed in the thought of somehow punishing the person who introduced the world to the seat belt extender. In retrospect we could all be living in Singapore where they "Cane," the guys who are overweight.

The Idea Factory

At Fit-Food the business was almost recession proof. In fact during recession it was good. I was of the belief that the entire diet industry was the brain child of Julia Child. First she got everyone into an eating frenzy and then she collaborated with companies secretly to create the diet food industry.

The job at Fit-Food was definitely not rocket science. It was not even science. All you had to do was reduce the volume of the regular meals by about two thirds and pack it in a fancy box. A billion dollar industry formed on a simple concept—eat less or create food that taste so bad people lose interest in eating.

The research team at Fit-Food had concluded that most obese people couldn't tell the difference between carbohydrates, fats and carbon dioxide. With the new healthcare policy implemented by the government the best solution was "death is cheaper than any healthcare plan" the effort was more towards elimination rather than prevention.

At Fit-Food one of my protégés was Mark Czubak a Russian immigrant. He was a big fan of Bollywood movies and truly believed my made up stories of knowing every

Bollywood star. Mark was one of my main innovators at the Fit-Food.

Mr. Frost hired Mark simply because of him being a Russian. He figured all Russians were rocket scientists. Mark, unlike most Russians, was not a rocket scientist. He was not a scientist either. He was clueless most of the time on most things, but had one advantage. His accent drove Mr. Frost up the wall and in order not to face Mark ever again he would nod to every proposal Mark brought in front of him. All proposals we created were delivered to Mr. Frost by Mark.

Lately, I had put Mark in charge of coming up with a new product line, diet food for obese vegetarians.

Mark had revealed to me that obese vegetarians were the fastest growing sector in the diet food industry. I was leery of every statement Mark made. How could vegetarians be obese? Sounded to me like an oxymoron.

I was aware of Mark making up all kind of statistics to make his argument, I had taught him that, but in this case he told me he was correct. He had validated the statistics with two of his vegetarian friends who were obese.

Henry, on the other hand, was fit. There were no fat people in First Class. I realized that the Donald was right in calling Rosie a loser. I could never imagine Alan Greenspan at 350 pounds or John Chambers at 400 pounds. They could still be intelligent at that weight but not successful. People magazine had an article about a kidney transplant being much cheaper in the U.S. than a nose job.

"B.S., what is your success rate for projects at Fit-Food?"

"It depends on what number the boss wants, we generally try to keep it low in accordance with industry average so we don't have to justify anything. But to be honest, I think it is around 30."

"Not too bad, but you could definitely do better than that. You need to focus on your definitions and justifications of projects."

"I am guessing the next napkin will have something to do with that I am assuming," I was focused on the napkins. E-bay was waiting for me.

"Yes, you are correct."

Some Projects Have No Purpose, Know Your Project

I believed in *karma*. Henry, I thought was talking about bad *karma* projects.

"Henry, are we talking bad karma project?"

"Not quite B.S., even though I do believe in *karma*. One of the early signs that a project is doomed to fail comes from an understanding of its status in the organization's priorities. The lower the priority of a project within an organizational strategy, the more the chances of a project failure."

"Henry, but that still doesn't sync with no purpose, are project priority and purpose linked?"

"Excellent question B.S., the purpose of a project has to be related to an organization's strategy and purpose. Sometimes there is not a convincing argument for a project to go on and yet it is approved for the wrong reasons."

"Henry, if I was to follow your principle, I would have to shut down all the projects, the only purpose of most of the projects we run at Fit-Food is to keep our jobs. It is not part of any organization strategy."

"I doubt to differ, B.S."

A lot of things that happen in nature have no purpose at all except for religious fanatics. I was sure of that. What is the purpose of snow? Mess up the folks of North Dakota into killing each other as a hobby? What is the purpose of a spelling bee competition? As a child I had to spend long summers doing nothing but memorizing the Webster dictionary. No wonder I became a History major instead of an astronaut.

At Fit-Food a lot of projects had no known or unknown purpose. They were essentially the "stimulus plan for project managers."

"Henry, why would you call a project with no purpose a project? How does one approve a project with no purpose?

"B.S., not all projects are approved as a strategic initiative even though in theory that is the definition of a project. Projects are justified and approved based on a company's needs, based on a sponsor's needs, based on internal politics and based on creation of a perception for the stakeholders. There are many ways a project can be justified."

"What's wrong with that? Why would you even worry about projects with no purpose?"

"For the simple reason that projects with no purpose, need to be analyzed and acted upon as projects with no purpose. You need to protect your resources and reputation dealing with projects with no purpose. A project with no purpose can definitely be a project with expense."

If people like Henry can recognize some of the projects they have executed as "projects with no purpose" the field of project management was indeed looking very fuzzy. It had taken my staff almost six years to differentiate between a project and an operation and I don't think I would be alive when they would understand the difference between project with purpose and project with no purpose.

In the South, people didn't see much purpose for having a full set of teeth. How could they understand the significance of a project with no purpose? I had to write myself a note to get out of the South quickly.

Henry must have observed the puzzled look on my face "B.S., operations can be mistaken for projects in certain cases. Improvement schemes many times disguised as projects can use up valuable time of resources strategizing. At Fit-Food you must focus on this difference."

At Fit-Food I was focused on early retirement. Early retirement due to lack of challenge in any activity related to the brain. Sometimes, it seemed that the workforce at Fit-Food resembled all the lazy lions resting at the Krueger National Park.

THE SOFTER SIDE OF ESTIMATION

The journey to Los Angeles had become a pilgrimage for me to the land of knowledge. I also had become appreciative of Henry's providing me with knowledge in small doses. For the first time I understood why communication involved listening. I had never listened so patiently in my life. Listening was no longer boring to me.

I was also surprised to see Henry not getting into any sophisticated formulae or equations on the subject of project management. Was he leaving it out simply because he understood my incompetence in math?

The topic of estimation was one of my most hated subjects on the certification exam. If they ever allowed a single phone a friend option this would be it. Not that any of my friends had any clue differentiating between PERT, GERT and Nerd. They probably would have asked me "Is this a language question?" At Fit-Food estimation started and ended with padding. Lots of padding. I always believed that padding was to estimation what air-bag was to automobiles.

"B.S., a good project manager is also a good estimator, won't you agree?"

"Henry, I agree with you, I just can't cope up with the whole math thing."

"Being a good estimator has very little to do with math. Estimation has to do a lot with experience and perception."

Henry was right. If mathematics and calculus were so hot, Marcy in our packaging department would not be making more money than Andy Gross, the Ph.D. in Mathematics at the local community college? Andy however was married to Marcy once and that probably explained his love for numbers and dislike for humans. Marrying Marcy he probably had lost most of his marbles to negotiate anything.

Henry's thought number 10 was on the napkin.

Estimating Without Perceiving is a Waste of Time

"Projects need to be evaluated from multiple perspectives such as timing, profitability, strategy, service, etc. A project manager and his team are responsible for sensible estimates not theoretical estimates. Estimation is not a mathematical function, it is an experimental function. The more the team is involved in understanding the objectives of the project, the better the estimates."

I realized once again that Henry never lost track of the word "objectives." The beauty of intellects is that they can store key words right in front of them and pick them up whenever they needed to use them. For mere mortals like us, the retrieval of information had to be done through multiple sources and methods some of which involved a vigorous shaking of the head.

"B.S., you have to be familiar with estimation basics before you become good at estimating. One simple way of learning how to estimate is to follow your own track record. In most instances you don't need to get into any secondary or tertiary derivatives."

"Secondary and tertiary" were scary words for me.

Having lived in Georgia and Mississippi I had no chance of being anywhere close to being good in math or anything technical. Most of our teachers were in jail convicted of changing grades so that we could pass. An appropriate reward for being a good Samaritan.

"Henry, I thought the terms secondary and tertiary applied only to mortgages."

"B.S., the whole country is thinking secondary and tertiary mortgages, so you are in good company."

I was getting comfortable at Henry's suggestion that the purpose of estimation was to aim at reality without sacrificing innovation. Henry's consistent emphasis on practicality impressed me. His approach told me that his emphasis was always on the systems approach rather than islands of activities. No wonder Barnes and Noble was doing the biggest disservice to project managers making them read "how to" books blindfolded.

"B.S., projects fail because the estimates are tied to baselines which are tied to project objectives in a simple linear fashion. Estimations can never be linear in a project. There is no fixed relationship between project constraints."

"Henry, I am beginning to understand why most projects fail. It is becoming clear to me that in most cases, it is not the project managers fault, but the 101 fairy tales on project management that are being spread all over by academicians."

"B.S., what is with you and the academicians anyway?"

"Henry, I don't like the smirk on their faces."

"B.S., don't forget that a lot of my comments are around the term "perception." A team perceives how activities need to be estimated based on the controls set by the project manager."

"Henry, I believe it is called the Parkinson's Law. "

"B.S., you surprise me. You are very perceptive."

My good *karma* had finally been awakened. If Henry thought I was perceptive I had to be perceptive. My parents probably did comment a lot on my being perceptive when I was young but I could never understand their accent.

Once again Henry's few words on the napkin held more knowledge than the entire dummy series on management.

No one ever questioned the great estimation techniques used by Wall Street gurus until the U.S. started moving towards the "under developed country" status. I am still not sure if the world realizes that *greed* is not an estimation technique.

At Fit-Food the projects were always in need of superb estimating. Even before a new variety of diet food product line came out, the customer already wanted a change. The life cycle of most diet product line is inversely proportional to the waist line of the customer and hence short. No one tolerates "pumpkin pizza" for more than a month.

I couldn't reveal my true estimation technique to Henry. The way I conducted project estimates was fairly simple. I took the end numbers my boss provided me, multiplied them by 1.5 and eventually divided by 1.25 after so much haggling that my boss was convinced it couldn't be done any other way.

I did know the art of negotiation. It was part acting, part begging and a whole lot of smoothing. I knew Mr. Frost was uncomfortable with anything technical. I used to put a whole lot of Greek symbols in front of him just to scare him off. It worked every time. Sometimes I almost felt I was as good an actor as my hero Robert. I could have been somebody.

"Henry, why do we need terms such as optimistic, pessimistic and most likely in estimation?"

"Right once again, we don't need them. They were useful during the second world war, but not much now"

As a History major I had read a lot about the war more so in the form of the PS3 and X-Box literature than text books. The one good thing that I thought technology has brought to the world is video games. Imagine the poor Korean kids. What would they do without the video games? You could see the birth of a thousand Kim Jong II.

Mr. Frost would have thrown me out the first day on the job if I had told him that pessimistically the job could take forever or words like "who knows."

"B.S., are you talking to yourself?" Henry interrupted my thoughts.

"Estimation is a hated word around the workplace," I uttered showing a little frustration.

"Well exactly my point," Henry continued, "No one believes in numbers unless they are convinced it is practical to use them. Data and statistics need to be used with a lot of practical experience; they need to incorporate factors such as team reaction under pressure, material cost fluctuations over time and external factors."

"Henry is there a way to get better at estimation," I had to ask.

"B.S., I will send you some practical examples. Use it as a template."

I was impressed. Henry was sincere in whatever he did. I was hoping he would send me a translator to explain those templates.

Henry was not done with estimating yet.

"B.S., it is naïve to add a percentage of cost and time as buffers without understanding specific factors that affect a specific project. Think about a builder in this economy or an automobile company in recession or better yet the gas prices over the next four years, a better estimation technique would not have resolved these problems. It requires the understanding of systems and their correlation to time and other factors."

Henry was getting into an area that none of us at Fit-Food had gone before and probably liked it that way. There was no need to jump out of an airplane leaving the parachute on the ground.

OVER OPTIMISM=UNDER PERFORMANCE

My conversations with Henry led me to believe Henry knew how to read Southern people well. I was also aware that consultants by nature had to be good at communications.

I was also trying very hard to figure out what prescription I needed to become successful like Henry someday. Born of parents who were both successful medical professionals with a bad Indian accent, I should have done better. There had to be some smart genes hidden somewhere in my brain. How do I awaken those giants? I needed to read Tony Robbins again.

The topic of estimation had created several wrinkles in my cerebrum. The cerebellum was trying to fight the rivers of beers flowing into my body. I was hoping the second half of Henry's sermon would be about "how simple thinking is key to project success."

"Henry, what are your typical conversations with the President and his council at the White House," I had to ask.

I was hoping Henry could tell me stories about his meeting with the President of the United States. What did they talk about? How do you prepare yourself for a meeting with the President? What if you made a faux pas? What if you asked him a stupid question? What if he thought you were from the Fox News channel?

For a minute I thought Henry had dozed off. The meeting with the President was something he probably didn't want to discuss with me. The meetings probably were so boring just thinking about it gave Henry a headache.

"B.S., you are in deep thought. Did you want to ask me something?"

"Henry, I was thinking, you have talked with world leaders including our President. What do you guys talk about?" Inquiring minds had to know.

"Just polite stuff, your regular chit chat and an occasional deep dive into next generation technology, or the "green" impact. He is very easy to talk to," Henry was blasé about his meeting with the President.

Being part of the People magazine generation I knew a lot about celebrity life. I wanted more from Henry to write in my blog on Southern life or sudden death.

"Henry, who is the most interesting person you have come across in your life." I was curious.

"That had to be his holiness The Dalai Lama."

I thought his holiness the Dalai Lama was Richard Gere's Hollywood agent. Henry surprised me. I didn't think he was the religious type and yet the Dalai Lama was at the forefront of his thoughts.

"Why?" I had to ask.

"Because Buddha is not alive," he was revealing his softer side to me.

"B.S., I am shocked you haven't read much about his holiness the Dalai Lama's teachings."

"Henry, you are right. I have even been to his *ashram* in India with my parents, but at that age I thought they were taking me to another spelling bee camp. Also, living in the South, my general knowledge is limited to *ways of shooting darts*."

I felt stupid. Here I was of Indian origin, taught about the teachings of Buddha and Dalai Lama and million other Gods all my life and my entire brain was filled with the philosophy of Henley, Lennon and McCartney.

I promised myself to read up on Buddha and Dalai Lama as soon as I cleared my certification. That should provide me with at least three to five years of lee way before jumping into spirituality. The path from Bob Seeger to Buddha is not an easy one for any human being.

"Henry, you know a lot about Asian culture. Were you ever in India?"

"Yes, B.S., I have been consulting with the Indian Government for many years on infrastructure issues. A lot of my practical ideas come from my work in India. It is an amazing country."

I had never been to India in a long time. The fear of my parents tying me to a cow and getting me married prevented me from leaving the South. A woman with no teeth was definitely better than a cow with no job.

"B.S., the Buddhism philosophy is one of peace and happiness; you should follow it as a lifestyle."

My philosophy in God and all matters related to God was quite simple. I believed in all faiths, in all Gods, in all "Gurus" and in anything that claimed they were God. I didn't want to get up one day in Hell simply because I had prayed to the wrong God. I was strongly "In all Gods I believe" camp.

"Henry, how often do you find the time to read all these books and meet all these great people?"

"B.S., we can all make time for what we really need in our lives. For the past few hours you made the time to listen to me, you could be watching movies but you decided to hear some boring speech on project management from me," Henry once again surprised me with his modesty.

"Henry, this are the best two hours I have spent so far in my life learning something that no college professor could have taught me. You have the unique ability to keep me awake discussing a technical subject. No one has been able to do that before," I was enforcing discrete sucking up to the max.

"B.S., let's continue with our quest on making project management interesting. Please hand me the napkin."

The napkin was placed before Henry. I had my eye on his Mont Blanc. It had to be an expensive one. May be accepting *dowry* was not a bad idea after all.

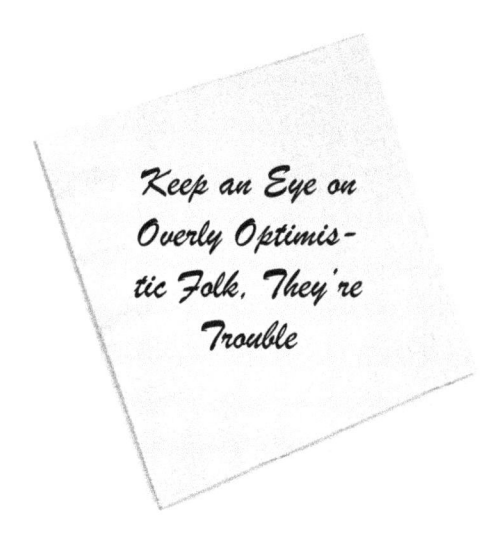

Keep an Eye on Overly Optimistic Folk, They're Trouble

"B.S., there is a natural tendency for project managers to please the customer. It is natural. Being overly optimistic is sometimes a result of insecurity."

"Henry is there a difference between the 125% success and over optimism?."

"That is a fair question. Being overly optimistic does not necessarily equate to aiming for 125% success. Being overly optimistic in most cases is simply ignoring the facts to the point of fault. "

At Fit-Food we did not have much of a problem with overly optimistic folks. The entire South had not been overly optimistic since the Civil War. The Fit-Food culture was more of overly ignorant rather than overly optimistic. The only relation I had in my life with optimism was during the playoffs where I would be overly optimistic about the Eagles winning the Super Bowl at least once before man landed on the Sun.

"B.S., managing a project in most cases is a tough proposition. The only way you can be successful is be confident in your own ability. Optimism stems from understanding several alternatives at once, over optimism stems from understanding no alternatives at once."

I had to constantly convince myself of being a good listener and to take it all in. I did see a yellow light stemming from my brain indicating I was getting closer to my memory being saturated.

For the first time in many years I realized there was a culture that existed beyond the "yes men" culture at Fit-Food. The "yes" men were my core group at Fit-Food. They created all kinds of regulatory documents to keep Mr. Frost worried at all times. That protected me from any harassment from Mr. Frost.

Henry's idea of coming up with alternative solutions to a problem sounded good but not feasible. How does one become an optimistic project manager with a set of alternative solutions? What would be an alternative to pumpkin salad? Paper Mache?

On the subject of overly optimistic folks, I remember Mr. Frost had this idea of a revolutionary product line called the Santa Diet. It would be our present to the obese folks during the Christmas season. For some reason we decided to put the picture of Nick Nolte in his jail costume as the diet Santa. The product was a sellout.

"Henry, Is there such a thing as overly optimistic folks in an era of recession," I asked.

"There are overly optimistic folks in every era. There are folks who never grow up."

"Henry is over optimism the same as over confidence?" I had to clarify.

"There is a difference between excess optimism and over confidence. Both are bad. However over confidence can be tolerated as opposed to excessive optimism. Excessive optimism leads to putting your guard down. Over confidence is sometimes a cultural or personality issue."

At Fit-Food the standard protocol for classifying all project managers was simply "an out of place idiot." The team was considered "too dumb to challenge anyone" and the operations folks were considered "pathetic to the point of no return." We had no issues of over confidence.

Working at Fit-Food over the years had made me gain a whole new respect for the term "mediocrity." I realized that mediocrity unlike other life styles was better in the long run. Most people I knew were in mediocrity heaven and they loved it. Mediocrity was a state of mind where *nothing* was an extension of your personality.

"B.S., you can be overly optimistic or overly pessimistic sometimes with projects, but keep the focus on long term objectives to succeed as a project manager and you will be all right."

"Optimism can be classified as a technical trait; being overly optimistic is a character trait. Problem solving ability stems from confidence, optimism stems from experience and attitude. Don't try to challenge nature."

Character and technical traits were good words and they probably meant no harm to anyone, but at Fit-Food life was a little different. The ability to focus on objectives disappears very quickly when you have folks who create a barbeque pit in the middle of the manufacturing facility. At Fit-Food most of the folks were on restraining order with respect to touching the factory equipment.

"B.S., once again it looks like you have disappeared into some deep thought, just remember Overly Optimistic folks can be trouble on projects, managing expectations is the key."

"Thanks Henry. I get it. I am just trying to put it all in perspective with the Fit-Food culture."

Henry was probably beginning to see the yellow light signaling the saturation point of my understanding. Darwin was so wrong. The theory of evolution has taken the shape of the bath tub. We have been flat for a long time. I was trying to shake my head to create some space for Henry's next thoughts.

Big "E"—The happening Formulae

Sooner or later the concept of earned value had to show up in Henry's approach to project management. I hated the concept of earned value. It seemed the term earned value was a combination of all the formulae rejected by mathematicians. What does it mean to earn it? Earned Value reminded me of the Old man in the ad—"You earn it." Why did you have to work hard to "earn friendship?" What kind of friendship is earned? In the South friendship is bound by lack of teeth or the love of beer.

Looked like everyone used it but no one had a clue as to why or how earned value was useful on a project. The common thing I heard at most of the conferences I attended was "you got to know earned value." The level of detail provided on earned value unfortunately ended there. The problem with mediocrity is that mediocrity breeds generality and generality is the mother of destruction. At Fit-Food most of the news came from the Yahoo columns including suggestions on running the projects. Unfortunately, our project managers misspelled a whole lot of things on the search engine resulting in us looking at all the forbidden sites most of the time.

I did realize that Henry had not checked his watch during the past two hours. He was confident he could not get a dime worth of consulting from me. He had to revert to his ethical duty on this one.

Henry's approach and attitude towards his profession was mind boggling to me. He was certain that "he did not know it all" but he was also certain that "he knew certain things for sure." I wish my parents had taken some lessons from Henry on raising me as a "project." The tools and techniques and the inputs they provided were boring as hell. Their accent and their attitude put me way deep in the South. I could have been a sure candidate for Ivy League.

Henry's Mont Blanc was once again on the quest of superior writing. I realized now how the twenty cents Bic had made a mockery of the art of penmanship.

Henry finally put me in trouble with napkin #12.

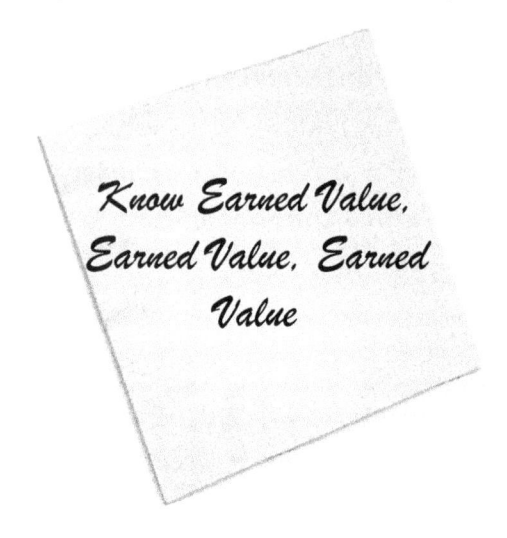

Know Earned Value,
Earned Value, Earned
Value

"B.S., my friend, do you recognize earned value"

I wouldn't recognize earned value if someone had a gun over me, but I couldn't act completely stupid.

"Henry, who wouldn't recognize earned value, I was wondering when you would bring it up."

From the few professional chapter meetings that I had attended that were not dominated by sales people I had learned that something big was going on with earned value.

At Fit-Food we had our own opinion about earned value. Jimmy from assurance figured earned value was simply created to "catch the liars." In Jimmy's opinion the whole banking crisis was not paying attention to earned value. Jimmy had raised the bar on earned value up another notch. Jimmy probably had no clue what he was talking about. He was simply repeating what he had heard.

The suffering one goes through when someone repeats something from the yahoo news column that has already been repeated a thousand times is probably the number one killer of mankind.

Living in the South though at times has its own advantages. Entertainment value is clearly one of them. I realized that there was a Southern translation for every project management term. I personally had heard about twenty different definitions of WBS and yet of the twenty definitions none started with the word "Work."

As the pseudo head of project managers at Fit-Food I was afraid to bring in new terms such as earned value. It was like bringing in a computer during the Roman era. You needed muscles not brains.

I was sure that earned value was a hyped up technique created by an academician wanting to publish that one extra paper to get tenured. My personal gripe against academicians has always been that they can simply add a "X" or a" Y" in front of a simple sentence and it becomes a new technique. Ever since I got all "Ds" in my sophomore year I hated academicians. Imagine repeating History courses again in college.

"B.S., no matter how you approach cost, scope or schedule on a project, you have to be consistent in your approach from project to project, do you agree?"

"Who am I to challenge you, I agree, Henry."

"Now, consistency leads to some form of standardization, and standardization are generally based on some best practice monitored over time. Earned value simply is the art and science of how costs are allocated to either activities or deliverables."

"Earned value is a sophisticated way of allocating costs to project deliverables. In many cases instead of evaluating individual variances, it is better to understand Earned Value."

"It can also be considered a way to understand the total impact of all variances together including cost, schedule, scope and quality," Henry continued.

"Henry, why do I need to know the hundred formulae related to Earned Value?"

"You exaggerate, my Indian friend, there are only 75 formulae."

"Exactly my point Henry, after the number five it is all hundred to me. I don't see why I have to memorize the formulae without understanding it."

"B.S., you don't have to memorize any formulae. The formulae simply state the variances from a cost or schedule perspective. They also indicate how the project will behave based on your improvement or lack thereof strategies to handle variances."

"Is there just one consolidate formulae for Earned Value?"

"Yes. It is called a template. I will be sending you a set of templates to set-up earned value for all your projects. You should have no problem calculating Earned value on any of your projects."

Henry was making my life easier. All I needed to hire was an installer of templates. In the South it was extremely difficult to find an installer of templates. Most installers were familiar with kitchen sinks. I might have to broaden my search to Mid-West.

FAILURE IS NOT ALL THAT BAD

The earned value lesson had created a brain overload, triggering a dumping of some useless information from my brain. I suddenly felt light. I could no longer think stupid thoughts. I was not yet to the E=MC something stage but I could see. I was ready to shout at the mediocrity in the coach section, "When I go out to conquer, don't remind of the people who have tried and failed before, for I am not a believer in glorified attempts, I am just a magician who believes in his tricks."

My head was spinning with new ideas. Henry's pouring some sense into my brain had filled my "idea quota" for the next decade. I was deciding how to approach the folks back at Fit-Food when I returned from Los Angeles. If I was their hero before I probably was "God" now with this new found wisdom. May be I could part the aisles at Fit-Food. I was getting excited and I just couldn't hide it.

I was also wondering if Einstein could prove his theory of relativity with just three alphabets E, M, and C, and a number, I could do better with more alphabets. I could figure out a way to make people in the South less ugly.

My brain was scanning all kinds of random thoughts; all of a sudden I understood some of the smart stuff my parents were hell bent on teaching me. I remember the poem they were trying to teach me when I was five:

Just another day

Is that the desire?

Is it too dark?

Or it seems that way?

The flight to Los Angeles was about to change my life. If a single encounter with someone like Henry could get me this excited about project management, imagine what the Dalai Lama can do for my soul? I was going to join the rehabilitation club for ignored project managers to ignite my spirit.

"Henry, who do you listen to get motivated?"

"Everyday folks, I am motivated by everything I see, I am motivated by the stories of firefighters who put their lives at risk to save a cat, I am motivated by a mother who works three jobs to provide food on the table for her kids, everything motivates me B.S."

"Henry, I was talking about the technical field," I had to correct Henry for a change.

"My hero is Milton Friedman; you should read some of his writings"

Surprisingly, I did know Mr. Friedman and his winning the Nobel Prize in Economics. My parents in addition to making me compete in the spelling bee had also forced me to learn the names of every Nobel laureate in the world. I was personally trying to locate Mr. Friedman for revenge at age twelve.

I could not figure out, how both my parents passed their medical degrees. They were nerds who besides reading books and books never realized the value of humor in a human life. For them humor came in the form of "I love Lucy" which like all other Indians of their age they watched it over a hundred times. Imagine the role of Lucy in today's youth era. Lucy had to be good but Lucy was no 50 Cents or Bruno for that matter.

"Henry, are you a big believer in statistics?" I had to change the subject before Henry asked me any questions on Milton Friedman.

"No, I consider statistics a necessary evil, to be handled with care."

I was fairly confused by the term statistics. In most of the project management circles that I circled, they used statistical tables as paper plates.

What does statistic prove? According to statistics only 30% of the projects succeed. What does this mean? Which idiot classifies his project a failure? Even the insurance companies tell you, don't admit to your fault. Why then project managers are hell bent on answering some stupid survey that says did your project fail? Is this is your first failure or every project you work typically fails? Why have you not been fired yet?

If anyone does not believe that statistics for the most part is useless, just ask Mr. Gore. He is still recounting every ballot. Statistics had clearly predicted him the winner.

Henry had laid out a strategy for me to understand project management in a manner I was comfortable with. His many subtle hints and read between the lines, I missed. I did however could read what was bold and beautiful on the napkin. Henry's next thought had made its way on napkin number thirteen.

"B.S., let's look at the project from a perspective of failure."

"Why not Henry? The story of my life."

Failure of
a Project is
Relative

"B.S., in my opinion there is no such thing as complete failure of a project. There is the effort, the completion of tasks, the hard work, the sincerity of work force and the need to succeed."

"Henry, that is true and then you are fired."

"Well, not exactly. Firing is a whole different ball game. People get fired due to many things. We don't fire our politicians even when they admit faults that are unacceptable even to a new born child."

"Henry are we talking about project failures as a measure of some specific criteria not being met based on a sliding scale?"

"Makes sense to me, B.S."

"It took some effort on my part to think that, Henry."

There is at least one thing I had understood about project failures working at Fit-Food. It took six months before anyone knew there were issues with the project. In the weight loss industry all projects are based on greed so a failure of a project is in reality good *karma*. May be Henry was implying failure of a bad project is good *karma*.

"B.S., I don't buy the concept that most project fail. Statistics look at relatively simple indicators such as cost, time and scope. It is a very simplistic approach to measure project success"

"Henry, I thought triple constraints were the essence of any project."

"That is old news B.S., the triple constraints are relevant, but what makes the project successful is when the need for which the project was created is satisfied. If the need is not satisfied, the project is a failure."

"B.S., the success of a project is always relative and so also the failure of a project. Unless you terminate a project due to some exceptional reason all projects are partly successful and partly a failure."

"The project success matrix simply can't be two dimensional where cost, schedule and scope are the only variances measured; there is the matter of ability, innovation, changes, trust and adaptability."

"Henry, to me the success of a project has to be linked to a pre-defined success criterion that no one ever defines."

"True, B.S., there has to be a mutual understanding of what a successful project will look like along with the levels of success. This has to be defined jointly by the sponsor and the customer and modified just as other changes throughout the life cycle of the project."

"Henry, you are thinking like a consultant. Who in the world today is interested in looking at success from anyone else's perspective except their own?" I had to add.

"B.S., don't be too pessimistic. People in general are always good. They want to do good things, productive things. Sometimes they are not clear what their roles are. This is the reason why good communication is so important to develop trust."

Henry was right. My best friends were still the same guys I trusted in college. The reason had to be quite simple. Trust is developed at a time when neutrality exists. I was finally thinking like Henry.

"B.S., don't over analyze anything. Just remember the basics. What you feel right, and is right, there is always a process to justify that."

The word process once again reminded me of the upcoming certification exam. May be I could have all the processes tattooed on my body; there can't be a law on not bringing your tattoo's with you.

I was shocked at the split personality of my thinking. On one hand I was thinking high thoughts with respect to Henry's teachings while on the other side I was thinking about tattooing processes all over my body. It does take an eternity for humans to grow.

CHANGE MANAGEMENT IS FOR CONSULTANTS

"Change," for a lack of better word was I always thought good. The way consultants drew up the processes leading to change was bad. I never quite got it. They probably never got it. It looked nice. I guess in every one's life there is an encounter with useless consultants. In spite of the millions of consultants existing on the planet it is surprising that consulting is never offered as a major at any University.

At Fit-Food we used consultants. We never really hired them. We made them write proposals after proposals, chatted with them about their methodology and ideas till they dropped dead. I believe some of these larger consulting companies have put us on their "hall of shame" wall.

At Fit-Food there was really no need for major change management. The culture was not changeable, the people were not changeable and the facilities were definitely not changeable. This was not a technical company, the projects were not that complicated. The only thing that was complicated was to capture the requirements.

We used "House of Quality" to capture requirements. However, with our requirements capture process the house generally burned down. When you have the customer and the sponsor trying to physically kill each other during requirements capture imagine what happens during closing. How do you convert something like "We need a new product that sells?" into technical requirements?

At Fit-Food Mr. Frost hated all changes. He had been successful at running a business without any consideration for quality, efficiency or technology.

Mr. Frost's logic on change management was well thought of. He believed that if the internal workings of the human body with respect to food never changed, there was no need for major research or technology to create new food, only new labels.

"B.S., what is the number one thought that comes to your mind when you think change?" Henry was curious.

"Elementary Dr. Watson, change is good for you."

"B.S., when you say change is good for you, you make the statement in 2-D, without any reference to the third dimension."

The South has never heard of 3-D. In the South to think beyond 1-D is evil. I honestly didn't know the two dimensions Henry was referring to. As a History major, we were taught everything in 1-D and that was move forward, the past is all messed up. Henry had finally confused me. My brain was in a "do loop" trying to find the three dimensions. I had difficulty viewing those 3-D pictures. I would squint my eyes for weeks and yet I could never follow the third dimension.

Where was I going to find the 3-D glasses to see change management from a 3-D perspective?

"Henry, to me change management is a topic most people understand in their own way. If changes are absolutely necessary they have to be implemented."

"B.S., the question is not about implementation, the question is about pre-implementation, avoidance and negotiations. Change management is a tough area for project managers."

"Henry, I thought change management is something the consultants help you with."

"B.S., I see your love for consultants, but the consultant generally focus on the improvisation of the steps, they are not as focused on project objectives as you are."

"Henry, are you saying change is not necessary unless something is improved by it."

"B.S., my thought exactly," his eyes lit up as he handed me the fourteenth napkin.

Change is bad for you unless it is Profitable

Henry had made me realize that "change is good for you" was a cliché used by the intellects to mess up the commoner. In my whole life change had done nothing but mess me up. I never wanted to move out of my parents' million dollar home but I had to. I never had any intention to be on my own two feet leaving my parents' Beamer but I had to, and I never had any intentions to bear the weight of Fit-Food projects on my shoulders but I had to.

Change is not good. It just happens. It happens generally for the wrong reasons. A 90 year old man trying to find a job in this recession is not a change for him; it is crude reality. Is he thinking retraining or one strike at God?

"Henry, does change mean $$$ sign all over for you?"

"Yes of course, but change is more than a $$$ sign, it is a continuum of $$$ signs for a consultant. But I still claim changes are mostly unnecessary on most projects provided the culture is developed."

I knew I had to shut my mouth. Consultants don't like to discuss their greed with anyone; they like to show passion for their work.

"Project managers need to discover the "sources" of changes on the project, convert it to risks and handle them as risks. Risks are easier to handle on a project than changes. Changes sometimes can change the concept of "rational" on a project."

"Henry, I realize that you are talking about being rigid on controllable changes and being flexible on changes stemming from customers' poor planning."

"Absolutely, in a global competitive environment the business model is changing. Today the profitability model has changed. It is simply the difference between the constant or reduced selling price minus the constantly trying to reduce the cost of running projects."

I realized Henry's point. I was never interested in a globally competitive environment. The South was my abode and except for China which we considered a suburb of Memphis I was going nowhere global with any business idea.

The good thing about living in the South was cheap labor. At Fit-Food we hired a lot of college interns and made them work twice as hard as the regular employees. They loved it. They didn't know any better.

Mike Romo was my intern. All he did was create Visio diagrams for projects. He had very little sense of logic but he was great at color coordination. He could make any diagram look good. He did all our annual reports. There was no logic in the annual report. The numbers were all made up but the diagrams looked great in color. We also sold our annual reports at the local Staples as coloring books for kids.

"Henry, is there a way to be pro-active with changes, as far as the customer is concerned?"

"B.S. that is an impressive question. The customer needs to understand the change culture within the project organization. The more he is aware of the process and the cost, the more he becomes pro-active in his approach to specifications."

"Henry, by any chance are we talking the House of Quality concept?"

"Something like that, but in a way that helps the customer understand his stated and unstated needs in advance."

"Thanks Henry. I believe I am ready for a change management consultant job."

"So is every fast talking car salesman."

Risk Owners are Idiots

The term risk was not a popular word at Fit-Food. The term risk owner did not exist at Fit-Food for good reason. Why would anyone in the right mind be a risk owner?

At Fit-Food, it was ironical that in some ways we were all risk owners. We were sure the building we were housed in had lead all over. Timmy and Marcus had confirmed it by tasting the walls.

In theory you would think there are risks involved with creating food for the obese masses. Mr. Frost however believed Fit-Food to be a risk free business. He had this belief that people go on a diet not to lose weight but to prove that on the first of the year, they too can make resolutions.

At Fit-Food we defined risk as "definite occurrence of dreaded event." Planning for risks never made any sense to me. I always knew my team. They were risk personified. If I couldn't predict their behavior how was I to predict the behavior of anything non-human?

"Henry, can one remove rust from human brains?"

"The human brain reacts to its environment. The more you make it work, the better it performs. We all do lose brain cells after our late teens."

Alex, I will take brain cells for 400. I was hoping for some Roto-Rooter formulae to remove the rust from all the brains at Fit-Food. I couldn't change the environment.

"Henry, do you believe in telepathy."

"Now you are talking my Indian friend. I knew you had the knowledge of telepathy. I am a big believer in telepathy. Why you ask?"

"Henry, a lot of things you have told me, seems it would go better if I knew telepathy. If I could see the results in advance, I could be effective."

"That would be psychic not telepathy. Telepathy would simply be a mode of communication without mouth or ears."

I knew I was good at telepathy. At Fit-Food most communications involved gestures, fingers and foot.

Henry had been very patient with a lot of dumb questions I was asking him. I was hoping he could give me some insights on how to be perceptive in recognizing problems before they happened. I always found that the difference between success and failure was timing. All successful people discovered the invasion of problems a little ahead of the dummies.

"Henry, what do you think about brainstorming? "

"B.S., as a project manager you are responsible for your team's motivation and work ethics. Brainstorming can remove a lot of barriers with respect to team communications. It is an excellent source to bring out ideas amongst team members."

One of the biggest headaches I had at Fit-Food was dealing with brainstorming sessions. Mr. Frost had this wonderful idea that brainstorming was a cheap way to make his employees productive. Every week I had to conduct brainstorming sessions mainly to collect gossip in the name of project improvements. Nothing could be worse.

Michelle Shaw was our adopted grandmother at Fit-Food. She knew nothing about anything except making greasy apple pies. She was our Quality Check technician and the main source of all customer food poisoning cases. Michelle's mission was to convert every brainstorming session into a pot luck dinner. The pot-lucks were responsible for converting all our ideas into burps.

"Henry, you got to attend one of our pot-luck brainstorming sessions. You will have firsthand knowledge on why the North won the Civil War."

"You are truly a History major, B.S. You know your history."

"No Henry. I don't know my history or geography for that matter, but I did stay at the Holiday Inn last night."

I suddenly realized that we were getting closer to landing in Los Angeles. Once in Los Angeles, Henry was going to take off so fast, faster than I could say history. I had to squeeze as much information I could from Henry.

Henry was already ahead of me. He had laid out the Risk thought on the napkin.

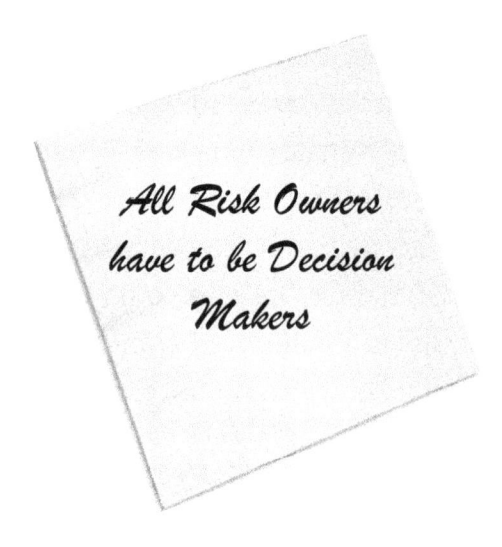

All Risk Owners have to be Decision Makers

"Henry, at Fit-Food we don't have risk owners, only risk creators."

"I see. Your team is definitely in the performing stage."

"You are right. We move from hiring to firing very rapidly. It is only because of Wendy in Human Resources that the fired people still have a year before they receive their official letter."

"B.S., risk is an important subject area for all projects. You mitigate risks, and you have a good chance of being successful on a project. You have to have a broad strategy on handling risks. How do you handle risks at Fit-Food?"

"Henry, I take one look at risk and stare it down."

My strategy to handle risks was the same as my strategy to handle everything else on the project. I used my influencing ability to let the team take care of it. It never worked.

"Is your team qualified to identify risks?"

I didn't know how many times I had to repeat the same old thing to Henry. My team was qualified for nothing. I considered them my potluck buddies and nothing else.

Most projects failed at Fit-Food due to our schedules created in Notepad. I believed we were the only company in the world to have schedules which had English sentences describing activity sequencing.

At Fit-Food it was considered politically incorrect to use words such as F-F, F-S, S-S and S-F. In the South any word starting with an F usually ended up with a K or a P.

Team motivation in my opinion did not apply to teams deprived of sleep. My team was extremely loyal to me but it didn't help. They were just not qualified to do anything productive.

At Fit-Food our process improvement seminars were conducted by Jane Murphy from Human Resources. Jane's husband had certified her as a very organized person. At Fit-Food a letter from a spouse was considered an authoritative fact on the employee's credential.

"B.S., you have to provide your risk owners the tools and techniques to make decision quickly. Risks not taken care of at the right time could lead to serious consequences later on."

The topic of risk was making me a little nervous. Henry's pointed questions on risks made me understand that I had to be proactive on risk issues and I was not the pro-active type.

I was also afraid that due to our lack of indulgence in anything related to good quality that we could be putting the diet consumer at risk. What if our ovens did not bake the food well? On several occasions we had discovered a soft copy of Mills and Boone in the batter. There were also complaints from Jane Murphy that library books were not returned for many months by several of our inspection team members.

"B.S., decision making is critical to a project manager. You have to learn how to delegate. In a complex project environment the people around you must grow. You have to train your people the rules of decision making."

"Henry, I hate to do this to you, but can you once again do a 1, 2, 3... for me."

"No problem."

Henry had become accustomed to my idiosyncrasies. He had no choice. You can't jump out of a plane at 35,000 feet.

Most human beings can't make decisions. Most married couples figure out within the first 24 hours of their marriage that their life is going to be hell together, and yet it takes an average of eleven years for couples to divorce. Most projects fail but it takes an eternity in most cases to fire the project managers. Thank God for that.

"B.S., the basic rules of decision making can be summarized as follows:

Every decision should have a clear objective

A decision can't be another puzzle

Decisions have to evaluate the practicality of adoption

Fair decisions never ruin friendships

A decision is not a commitment

A decision can't be easily reversed

A decision is not a judgment

Decisions need to be articulate

B.S., you can continue to add to this list."

"Thanks Henry. The list will be circulated at Fit-Food with my initials on it."

"B.S., have we discussed my consulting fee for this assignment?"

Thank God Henry was smiling. The only way I could compensate Henry for his consulting fee was to sell one of my kidneys.

"B.S., in part I agree with you with the term risk owner. The responsibility falls on everyone to come up with solutions, however, it is a responsibility and accountability issue. A risk owner has the task of resolving risks to the best extent possible."

The best extent possible at Fit-Food started and ended with crying. If you could cry from the moment you were assigned the risk to the point where you failed, you satisfied the "best extent possible" criteria.

Did Quality Kill the Japanese?

Quality was one of my favorite subjects. I never formally studied quality in college and struggled with statistics, but I was fascinated by the Japanese culture. It seemed everything related to quality was Japanese. I had visited Tokyo as a kid with my parents and was impressed by the bullet trains. My parents were impressed by the eighteen hour days kids put in school. I was too young to drink "Saki" but I am sure it would have been fun too.

My father was a believer in the "Zen" philosophy. He told me it was the best medicine for keeping one's blood pressure low. For an M.D. he had deep understanding of alternative medicine. May be he knew the truth about Western medicine. As a kid I was not sure of the connection between the Zen philosophy and quality, but I was sure it had something to do with the discipline factor. If there was one thing completely lacking at Fit-Food it had to be discipline.

"Henry, I need to know if there is any connection between the Zen philosophy and Quality."

"B.S., seems to me you are a practitioner of Zen philosophy."

"Does it work; if it works I will start practicing it."

"The Zen philosophy definitely works. It promotes the understanding of your surrounding and the oneness of everything in nature. It is a very peaceful and practical approach to living."

"Quality is relative to attitude and need. In many ways you can relate the Zen philosophy to quality. Everyone and everything needs to be involved for the greater good of product or mankind."

Henry was on target. All Indians were in sync when it came to quality. No Indian in the past decade has bought any other car except for a Honda Accord or a Toyota Corolla. It is easy to recognize Indians by their cars these days rather than their accent.

Quality, I felt, was an overused word. Mr. Frost believed quality was eating into our profits. He had no clue what quality meant to our business. Quality however provided him with one more avenue to squeeze additional work out of his employees for free.

At Fit-Food the struggle was to decide on what quality was. Mr. Frost believed quality was cost; the customer believed quality was taste, the quality assurance guys believed quality was Miguel, our genius technician, and the quality control guys believed quality was randomly throwing away 10 boxes out of every 100 boxes we made of anything. I believed the customer definitely could not complain about the 10 boxes we threw away every night.

Even to this day most of the quality folks at Fit-Food believe that Malcolm Baldridge is two people, Malcolm and Baldridge, Malcolm the actor and Baldridge from the refrigerator company.

"Henry, I am just fed up of superficial quality talk. Everyone talks about quality but it really should boil down to the customer willing to pay for quality."

"B.S., it is not just about the customer. Quality also reduces your overall cost over a period of time and increases profitability. Think about your reputation as a quality powerhouse. Think about what reputation has done for Toyota."

"Henry, there are too many terms coming out of the Quality field every day. Can we not just fit everything in one word continuous improvement?"

"Continuous improvement is only part of the quality philosophy, you need design innovation, simplified designs, supplier partnership approach, culture change and a whole lot more to implement good quality processes."

Surely, Henry was thinking defects per million opportunities and I was thinking survival at maximum defect level.

"Henry, what would you consider quality attributes in the diet food industry."

"B.S., quality attributes in your industry could be with respect to the raw materials, food processing, purity, processes, packaging, weight and a lot more."

"I believe you are right. We have issues in a lot of the areas that you mentioned. However, we are not as sophisticated to implement an automated measurement and control system."

"B.S., you got to look into using a DMAIC model super imposed on your project plan."

"Henry, who constructs this structure?"

"B.S., you can be the hero at Fit-Food."

I knew I wasn't invincible in quality, but Henry was tearing me apart.

I wanted to tear apart everyone who spoke about quality at Fit-Food. Our suppliers gave us the talk on how we could benefit from their six sigma programs and we bought into it. We received the same old defective materials with a promise of six sigma quality in the future. The suppliers were not six sigma certified, they were not even ISO 100, however they probably did stay at the Holiday Inn the previous night.

"B.S., let me put a simple but important thought about quality on the napkin."

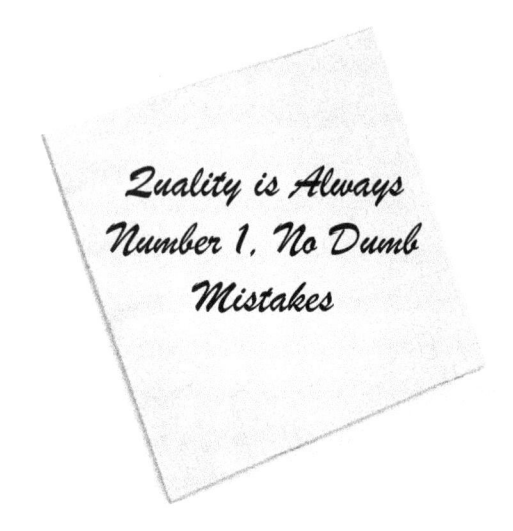

Quality is Always Number 1, No Dumb Mistakes

It seemed that Henry was thorough with quality. I couldn't figure out how. Does a project manager need to know so much about quality?

"B.S., as a project manager you are not supposed to be a subject matter expert on quality, however as a project manager you need to understand the concept of quality with respect to customer acceptance."

"Henry, what does the term "quality is number one" mean anyway."

"B.S., it is simply an expression of human emotion with respect to expectations. It could be a combination of functionality, feeling, perception or specification."

At Fit-Food it was difficult to invite quality consultants. The last quality consultant we had hired was thrown off the facility in less than an hour.

Joe Miller was a consultant I had known for some time. In spite of his reservations working at Fit-Food I had convinced him that he could help us with our quality program. It took him less than an hour to state, "You guys need to shut down the plant, your quality sucks." I always thought it was the taste of our food but according to him it was quality. Mr. Frost had him thrown out.

"Henry, all these companies I read in the newspapers have great quality products, but they do go bankrupt. What is the logic?"

"Quality is not the product. Quality is only an attribute of a product. You could have a wonderful product in your hand and not know how to market it. There are things beyond quality in business."

Listening to Henry made me realize that the more I began to understand about project management the more my life was going to be turned upside down. Ignorance was bliss and I was being enlightened.

"B.S., you need to hire a good quality person with a solid six sigma background and your troubles will melt away."

Where in the South was I going to find such a person? I would have to go over six states to add up all the single sigmas.

The Customer is Either a King or an Idiot

The four hour plane ride was looking like a two year internship at Henry and Company. I had never heard anyone so patiently. I was hoping that my brain was able to process at least half the information it received. That would make me the second smartest guy in the South after Larry, the cable guy. At Fit-Food most of the cubicles had the pictures of Larry or Foxworthy. They were the Malcolm and Baldridge of the South.

Henry's practical approach to solving project problems was appealing to me. I was also beginning to understand the pain of my team members working on projects. They had no clue what a process was. Without any form of standardization they had to re-think processes on every project they worked on. The only tool and technique they knew of was the Wal-Mart calculator. How does one create a Gantt chart on a Wal-Mart calculator?

I had my work cut out. I knew history repeated itself at Fit-Food. But the repeating history had to be repelled. I had an urge to call Timmy and tell him to get the troops lined up. There was going to be a whole new approach to managing projects from now on. Fit-Food was going to be a feel-good company from now on. A project manager had to do what a project manager had to do.

"B.S., seems you have gone into your meditation state."

"Henry, sometimes I get lost in my thoughts, when they are not coordinated."

It probably was a long time since Henry sat next to an Indian with ties to Borat.

I wanted Henry to get into the topic of customer. The word "customer" was hated at Fit-Food. We really didn't know who the customer was. Mr. Frost told us "he" was the designated customer for all our projects. We thought he was an idiot. There were signs posted all over the Fit-Food facility "The customer is King" after the local barber had gotten rid of the sign. All signs carried a picture of a comb and a scissor.

"Henry, which idiot coined the term "customer is king?"

"I believe the first businessman who was afraid of calling his customer by any other four letter word."

Henry shocked me. He was dead on. That was my exact thought. I always knew that the truth about calling the customer a king was something cynical.

"Henry, why do we spend so much time on coining terms which have very little value?"

"B.S., you have a valid point here. However, remember people and ideas evolve with respect to treating the customer. The whole concept of business is always around making money. The customer is the one who makes you that money. He has to be the king."

"Henry, today's customer is broke. He has acted like a king for so long he is now flat broke. We should all treat our customers like a liability, a check about to bounce."

"B.S., I thought in the Indian culture the customer is considered God."

Henry was hell bent on teaching me about the Indian culture. It was difficult for me to comprehend any other culture after living in the South for many years. My parents had even asked for a witch doctor from India to return me to my Mid-West roots.

"Henry, the thing that troubles me, is why do academicians feel the urge to write a new book on management each day? Isn't there a law against boring the commoner to death?"

"I see. You are talking about Chinese torture. I do agree with you, a lot many books are not worth the read. You should subscribe to the Harvard Business Review."

"I could Henry, but they need references."

I had figured that the person reading all the Management books at Barnes and not so Noble had to be unemployed. He most likely had not mastered the art of discrete sucking up and hence unemployed. Some people never get it; the time to read books is when you are on the job and not out of it.

At Fit-Food we encouraged employees to read books on the job. We believed that by reading books, they would have less time to spread rumors. In the South, they teach rumors as a second language. Most affairs in the South are a direct result of politicians being afraid of the rumors. If you are going to be destroyed by rumors might as well put some truth in it.

Our customer service representative at Fit-Food was Mike Patel. Only God knew the origin of his name Mike. We hired Mike, since he was a Patel. In the South the Patel's were considered the number one motel owners and hence the pride of the South. Mike really needed an attitude transplant. He had suffered with his bad attitude all his life, and now he was our customer service representative.

No one understood Mike. He had such a thick accent; you could hide the entire English language underneath it. Good news at Fit-Food was that complaining customers were scared of having any sort of conversation with Mike. I guess it is not difficult to understand why all mobile support for customer service is handled by Indians out of Bengaluru.

"Henry, what are the traits of a good customer?"

"A good customer knows what he wants, at the price he considers fair and has considered alternatives."

"Henry, I believe you are talking an informed and an uninformed customer?"

"You don't need to gold plate information when dealing with the informed customer. When it comes to customer, less talk is always better."

At Fit-Food more talk was better. We believed in the art of exaggeration. Our diet products were always part food and part exaggeration. If the 400 pound women wanted to get into the sleek bathing suit by being on our diet, it would take her exactly 40 years. We did not subscribe to the truth in advertising club and hence were immune from lying to the customer. In return the customer loved us.

"B.S., here's a thought for you to chew upon," Henry finally figured I was needing some help on customer issues.

Follow Customer Patterns on Compliments and Criticism

"The customer has certain traits that you need to understand and adjust in order to manage his expectations and generate a trusting relationship," Henry continued.

"Henry there is so much written about customer satisfaction that I hate the thought of reading anything more on the subject," I had to be clear about my frustration.

"I see, you believe you can't learn anything from reading books?"

"Henry, I don't like to read any books for that matter. I like to hear people directly. That cuts a whole lot of useless description."

"B.S., you are going to put me out of business. If all my potential customers follow your advice, I could be looking for a job at Fit-Food."

"Henry, I promise you I am going to buy all your books including the one you are going to co-author with me, as long as you sign those books for me," I had to add.

I had no experience of an author signing a book for me; most authors don't sell enough books to sign for anyone. The only author I ever had the opportunity to meet was the author of the dummy books for gardening. Unfortunately, someone mistook him as a bum at Barnes and not so Noble and threw him out of the store.

"B.S., a customer's criticism can be logical from his perspective, but his perspective can grow immensely from understanding the product from a project manager's perspective."

"Remember B.S., the project manager is responsible for creation of the product. He has seen all the improvements, limitations and attributes of making the product from up close."

Henry was probably talking about the project manager being a learning tool for the customer in making the product better. You never know what the geniuses are thinking. One minute you think you know them, the next minute they are encircling Mars.

"B.S., the field of project management has not emphasized enough on the project manager's role as a partner in the improvement of the product development process."

"Henry, are we talking value analysis."

At Fit-Food, learning new things was an attribute of the conferences we attended. Most of us picked conferences that were located on the beach. The topic honestly didn't matter. Most of these conferences probably had a speaker but we didn't know. We were generally stuck in traffic on the beach.

"Impressive, B.S., I didn't know you were fond of value analysis."

I was fond of pizza and that was the truth. Anyone working at Fit-Food was bound to be fond of pizza after eating at the Fit-Food cafeteria which should have been the grazing ground for cows.

To me value analysis was just another buzz word academicians coined as a requirement for tenure.

At Fit-Food we did have our value added expert. According to Julie Fettig, our production supervisor, value analysis started with Darwin. Darwin she said coined the term value analysis to differentiate humans from rodents. Humans added value, rodents didn't. Julie however also believed that the British won the Civil War.

"B.S., the key to managing customer expectations is to formalize every concern or criticism of the customer into quantifiable parameters. Anything that can be measured can be understood and improved upon."

"Henry, how do you quantify customer's gestures?

"B.S., the key to a good project manager is to remove the fear of anyone raising concerns on a project. The maturity of an organization always lies in its approach to resolving tough problems."

At Fit-Food, Mr. Frost knew how to please our most important customers. Samples of our "evergreen diet line products" were always presented to the customer at Morton's Steakhouse. The customer loved the steak at Morton's and forgot about the diet products they were holding. The only problem we encountered was the restaurant's general manager. He hated watching us demonstrate the diet product line in front of his cow chewing audience.

"Henry, you truly believe in treating your customer as your partner, in good times or bad."

"You got it B.S., there is no fear when the project manager—customer relationship is honest."

Outsourcing is not a Fad

Living in the South has its own advantages. The Southern edition of Webster's dictionary has only ten pages. The word Bubba is pronounced six different ways. ISO 9000 had to reduce the 9000 by three digits to get the support of the South. South has the only Mercedes Benz plant in the world with two Waffle houses located inside it. Every Mercedes Benz you bought from the South smells of them waffles.

At Fit-Food we were afraid of the word outsourcing. We didn't quite understand it. Most folks at Fit-Food believed it meant not hiring blood relatives. To others it was the use of computers.

At Fit-Food we outsourced all our intellectual functions. The formulae for our diet food were a closely guarded secret, not by us, but by the guys who stole the formulae and ran away to China.

Personally I liked the whole concept of outsourcing; It allowed us to focus on more interesting things such as Sudoku. We encouraged Mr. Frost to outsource most of our service functions after visiting a lot of industries where outsourcing had led to regular employees becoming regional Sudoku champions.

I always believed in America. If America felt outsourcing was good it had to be. We were the ultimate at taking advantage of the world. If we felt outsourcing was right than it had to be right.

The one place I would thing outsourcing would not be successful would be the suicide hotline, the accent of the operator would kill the person before they attempted the actual suicide.

"B.S., is any of the work at Fit-Food being outsourced?"

It was tough to answer Henry's question. We didn't quite understand what work went on at Fit-Food. On top of it, Mr. Frost had probably a lot of employees working under minimum wage, I guess that would be outsourcing too. On top of it we probably had employee represented from every country where there was a coup. Fit-Food would hire anyone who had one form of I.D. and a Visa or a Master Card and would accept less than the minimum wage.

"Henry, I believe it is 25% if not more," generating numbers from air was not new to Indians.

"That is quite significant. I bet you probably run into some tough issues."

I wouldn't know tough issues if the entire Stone Mountain collapsed on me. I didn't know why outsourcing was a tough issue. Most of the people we outsourced to never got paid. We were the pioneers of I.O.U.'s before it became a fashion statement in Kalifornia.

"B.S., here is my thought on outsourcing."

The Mont Blanc once again didn't deceive Henry. His immaculate writing once again reminded me what a Mont

Blanc can do to your soul. Imagine Shakespeare writing "To be, or not to be," with a twenty cent Bic.

Outsourcing is Risk Magnified

Outsourcing to me was simply a way for all those developing countries to seek revenge on the Western world by providing low quality goods at low prices and attempting to recover some more money by using "oops I am going to miss the deadline unless you pay me more" technique.

Henry was telling me nothing new on outsourcing. I had firsthand experience of outsourcing problems at Fit-Food. Mr. Frost had outsourced our website maintenance to the cheapest programmers he could found in Bangalore. If we wanted to curse the Indian programmers on the lousy job they were doing we had to get up at 2 in the morning just to curse them . . .

"Henry, outsourcing is risk magnified, is there something more to it than what I am thinking, which is simply—yes."

"B.S., you are right. There is nothing hidden in the statement 'outsourcing is risk magnified' I was trying to give you some insight into how even after knowing that outsourcing is risk magnified project manager's falter."

"The reason there is considerable risk with outsourcing stems from mistrust with the action of outsourcing. From the very beginning there is a sense that the reason one has to outsource is simply to save money and hence something will eventually have to give."

"Henry, I always thought outsourcing was a U.N. mandate to help out the poor nations, we were getting too fat."

"B.S., are you a U.N. fan?"

"No Henry. If you must know I am a Green Day fan."

"So you too have caught the green revolution."

I was sure Henry had no clue of what the music scenario looked like since the 50's.

"Henry, I am always skeptical of sub-contractors, they would never be loyal to my project. They are only loyal to the H-1B Visa. What would be their motivation to do anything beyond necessary? Why would they excel? How would they ease my problems?"

"Exactly the wrong thinking. They have a lot to lose than you do. They can only ruin part of your project, but you can do severe damage to their reputation. They have to work hard to convince you of their excellence."

"Henry, do you belong to the outsourcing union by any chance."

"No, I can't afford to. I am a consultant and hence can't discipline myself to be loyal to anyone."

For a nerd Henry was funny. Nerds are generally not funny unless you ask them a math question. As a kid my parents made me befriend only nerdy kids, a fact that all the other parents hated as their nerdy kids learned words that were not exactly asked on the spelling bee.

"Henry, is there a simpler way to reduce the risk with outsourcing?"

"Yes. The approach has to be from a perspective of need and excellence. If outsourcing is considered a tool to actually reduce the impact of a problem to your project, it makes life easy to work with the contractors. It should never be viewed from the perspective of money alone."

"Henry, are we talking Maslow here."

"Who is he? I am only kidding. No, Maslow generalized the human behavior with respect to maturity. I believe he didn't want us to outsource the pyramid called the hierarchy of needs."

I am sure Maslow had nothing much to do. Which person proposes that money is a low level need? If Maslow ever roamed New York he probably would be arrested as a bum.

"B.S., there is a reason life has gotten better for many due to outsourcing. Things are in many ways better because of outsourcing. However, you can argue about it all your life."

"I hear you Henry," I had to cool Henry down.

How Critical is the Path?

The fear of passing the certification exam was driving me crazy. I had heard that no one, who had not been an "A" student in college, had ever passed the certification exam. My grade point average in college was so low I had to use a microscope to view it. The only reason I actually graduated was the instructors could not bear a student who went on a hunger strike to die in front of their office.

The thought of answering network diagram questions on the certification exam scared me. I could never figure out the beginning or the end of the network diagram unless it said "start" and "end" and could never tell if it was upside down.

Neither could anyone else at Fit-Food. Network diagrams were great for the railroad companies but for the Fit-Food company we needed people diagrams.

I always thought the nerds had gone too far with the network diagrams. When humans no longer believe in relationships what is the need for defining network diagram relationships such as FF, FS, SS, and SF? What kind of a relationship is SS? What kind of a bar discussion that could be? Are you a SS project manager or a FF?

"Henry, what is wrong with world? Why do we have SS, FF and these two letter acronyms?"

"B.S., you don't need to worry about any other relationship except finish to start. Most of the activities on a project have a finish to start dependency anyway."

My whole life was a start to no end relationship. Most of my friends had "not knowing where to start" relationship, and most of the people at Fit-Food had "I know where it will all end" relationship. I truly didn't have the heart to disappoint them with the finish to start relationship when on most projects we had a "let's at least get it started relationship."

The worst part of my life was that even with very little knowledge and intelligence I was at the top of the intelligence pyramid at Fit-Food. I was the "guru" working on half empty. I had no place to go for truth or advice. I was living in a fantasy world where even fantasies were mediocre.

"Henry, do all network diagrams converge on a point," I had to finally ask a dumb question.

"Only if you want to complete a project, all things eventually end on a project. Remember the definition of the project—temporary."

No wonder. All our network diagrams, the ones we didn't outsource, looked like fountains. All the network diagrams we outsourced had food stains on them or could be they were milestones. I could never tell.

"B.S., the key to project success is to understand the critical paths. What constitutes them, how to resolve them."

The concept of critical path was not clear to me. I was hoping Henry would use the "text" version of his skills database to clarify the concept.

It was time for the nineteenth napkin to meet the fate of being sold on E-Bay.

There is no Single, Critical Path

There is no single critical path. I thought Henry had flipped on this one. It was a statement in plain simple English. I liked simple.

At Fit-Food we outsourced "find the critical paths on a project" to India. They charged us by the number of critical paths they found. We had more critical paths than the audience at the unemployment line.

The word critical path made no sense to me. What is so critical about missing a deadline? Everyone misses one. What is so critical about the longest path? I was always taught that in the hare and the tortoise story, the tortoise is the smarter one. We had pictures of the tortoise all over at Fit-Food.

Critical project—Yes; Critical path—No.

"B.S., I am sure you have fought many fires in your years as a project manager," Henry once again tried to jumpstart my brain cells, from a state of constant rest.

I was thinking, *Mothers don't let your kids become project managers.*

"Henry, first I have to admit I don't consider myself a real project manager, and second, I am generally extinguishing fires which have already burned the house down," my frustration was showing.

"We all have gone through that, B.S., there is no peace for any project manager in most of the projects, but it can be better."

I had to agree with Henry. Life for me could only get better. I couldn't gain any more weight unless I was dead, I couldn't find a worse job, starting from zero had its own advantage. If the Slum dog can become a millionaire I was definitely in a much better position.

I had taken my project team to several positive thinking seminars. We came back even more depressed. The problem with positive thinking was, it lasted no more than two hours, than you realized you were living in the South.

The one thing I enjoyed about my job as a project manager was I could always find time to take a nap; this is what I called "Kaizen." Kai meaning to take a nap and Zen meaning rejuvenated. Taking a nap rejuvenated me. I believe the Japanese also have a similar philosophy.

"Henry, I thought all projects have multiple critical paths. What's wrong with that?"

"B.S., most project managers practice the art of managing a single critical path at a time. The art of "fire fighting" stems from creating a chaotic environment in the first place by assuming one can control multiple paths by focusing on one path at a time. This is not true."

"Henry, at Fit-Food if we could multi-task we would try to find another job."

"Human beings by default are capable of multi-tasking. In project management, project managers are unaware of the importance of systems. Systems are not simply constraints, but a true relationship amongst and within deliverables."

"Henry, I have heard the word systems many times. Is it a technical concept, or a man-made technique?"

"B.S., it is a technical concept, with management implications. To understand the systems approach to running projects is important to smart project managers."

"Henry, how does a project manager keep up with all these concepts of self-improvement? There are only eight working hours in a day."

"It is not the hours B.S., it is just constantly evaluating things that work for you and improving upon things that don't."

"I see. Just like the entrance of Blu-Ray and the death of DVDs."

"Exactly, I guess."

I had this effect on people. They couldn't call me outright wrong. They had to use the smoothing technique. Henry was no exception.

"B.S., my simple theory on critical path is that the critical path is not a constant entity, but an ever changing entity, that should be observed at a given point in time. What is critical at the beginning could be resolved in mid-stream and so forth."

I had no clue what Henry was talking about. The signal receivers on my brain imitated the AT&T wireless service. You never knew when the signal would disappear.

Henry I was sure was not a big believer in constant data, he probably believed in the dynamics of activities within a project. Critical path was a derivative of time and situation within a project that arose when priorities changed within constraints.

The thing that made me happy was the fact that critical path was not a formulae but something I could talk without making sense to my team.

THE CLOSING THOUGHT

The flight to Los Angeles was an eye opener. The luxury of sitting in First Class along with people who didn't consider Sears their style "guru" had a tremendous impact on my attitude. I was wrong, the rich people were not only intelligent but they knew project management better than I. No wonder the mouth of the South lived in Florida.

Henry had not stopped chatting with me for the past four hours and was sincere in his approach of sharing knowledge and experience with a project manager who was a complete stranger to the field of project management.

I was already thinking about how to incorporate all of Henry's tidbits in my day to day handling of people, projects and customers. Mr. Frost would probably be the single most beneficiary of my meeting with Henry. He would just tell everyone that it was "He" who had sat next to Henry and taught him a thing or two about the weight-loss business.

There was still the question of the last napkin. What would Henry write as his concluding thought on project management?

So far, I had understood a lot about running a project from Henry. I was hoping he would give me some tips on the closing process. I had read the Donald's art of the deal, but he didn't really explain the closing process. The entire book was about his ego and the different layers of it. He was the perfect anti-Maslow.

Closing a project at Fit-Food was pure hell. As a project manager I was not qualified to know about the legal terms attributed to closing.

To me the terms SOX and Cubs both meant the losing teams of Chicago. The term GAAP meant the difference between customer expectations and project delivery. I knew that the closer the project came towards the end the bigger the GAAP.

Mr. Frost had however a different perspective on closing. He wanted me in charge of closing all projects. He believed that as an Indian I was good at accounting principles or better yet as his loyal project manager I would surely not make him look bad in front of the SEC.

At Fit-Food closing was where all outstanding issues came to life. After hiding most of the issues under the rug throughout the project, closing was where we had to reveal them. Closing was also the time when our customers handed us the print out of all issues that had been raised and ignored by us.

I was a believer that closing should never take place face to face. Sometimes the "face to face" is not a smart idea. There are faces which are so ugly you forget what the real issues are. There are faces that are so lifeless you can't read anything from it. When academicians say that most communications is non-verbal they are talking about those faces. Nobody can stand talking to those nerds and hence for them all communications is non-verbal.

At Fit-Food the ceremony of closing was real scary. The customer generally came with an attitude of opening, "Swearing in" comments. Instead of saying a prayer and holding hands we were generally targeting the throat. Closing in the South generally happens when the cops show up.

Mr. Frost had an unusual impact on customers at closing. They all wanted to punch him. I wanted to punch him. My whole team wanted to punch him. He generally felt that the purpose of every project at Fit-Food was to make him poorer. It was like he was giving away the product for free.

At Fit-Food the thought of closing started from day one and was thought about throughout the project. We believed closing came before initiation.

"B.S., let's get to the topic of closing. What are your thoughts?"

I was on top of the world. The great management "guru" was asking me about my thoughts. I had to summon my wandering brain to jump start the "creation of thoughts" machine. Sometimes one feels cheated by the brain. You expect a lot from it and yet it fails to deliver. I believe it simply needs a stimulus package just like everyone else.

"B.S., here is my thought on Closing," Henry scribbled something on napkin #20. I was about to cry. This was going to be the end of the conversation Henry and I would ever have.

Henry probably was at a point cursing his travel agent. He probably would have been happier in the coach section, talking with idiots who could never recognize anyone except their local grocer or Oprah. No one would have bothered him.

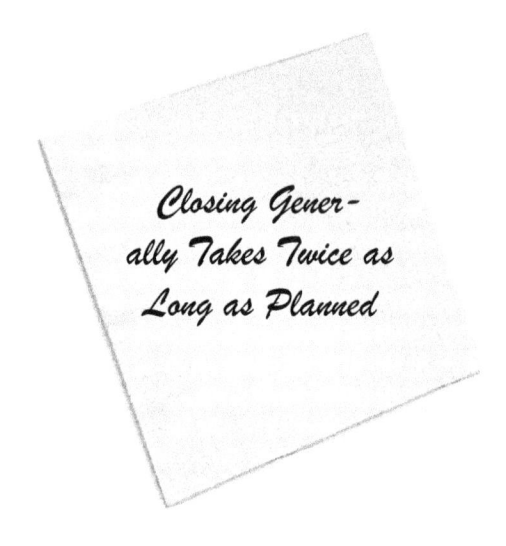

Closing Generally Takes Twice as Long as Planned

"Henry, closing takes twice, may be three times, but what significance does it hold," I was getting bolder.

In the art of the deal the Donald does mention wearing a nice suit during closing.

"Nothing really, just that when you think about closing you need to understand, it is a process unlike the previous processes."

"You mean it is not part of a project," I had to ask another dumb question. I realized what I had spoken but at this time my brain and speech had divorced each other.

"No, B.S., it is part of the project alright. Closing is where bringing together the sponsor or the customer with the reality of accepting your work happens. It requires a long effort to gain his trust and understanding."

"I get it Henry. Closing if not planned properly can turn ugly and can unnecessary increase frustration whereas it should be a time for celebration"

"B.S., you should have been a poet."

"To be or not to be, occurred in my life several times Henry."

"Closing for a lack of better word is an art, B.S. One who pro-actively works with the stakeholders to manage expectations at all stages succeeds in simplifying the closing process. This is where understanding the customer's requirements from the beginning and managing it does help."

"Henry, what do I do with the "twice" factor?"

"You just plan for twice the time that you normally factor in for closing activities. You also need to adjust for it in your overall project estimation."

I was a true believer in closing. I liked God's model for closing. No matter who you are or what you are, when it is closing time your chapter is closed.

The classic lessons learned theory that works for projects does not work for human beings. Human beings never change. There is no Botox for human behavior.

"B.S., closing requires the coordination of all documents that are approved and an understanding of open issues that don't end up as show stoppers."

"Henry, what if the customer is hell bent on creating trouble during closing?"

"B.S., there is a natural tendency for any human being to negotiate the very best for his organization. Closing is the last step in the project and hence if you can negotiate some favors at the end, more power to you."

"Henry, are you saying it is natural to fight during closing?"

"No. It is natural to maximize your leverage at this point. This can be done very professionally. No different than closing on your house."

I wouldn't know that. The only house I could think of closing in was the million dollar house I was going to inherit from my parents. But since they were healthier than me, the chance of that happening was extremely slim. On top of it, the whole South was community property, so owning a house in the South didn't make any sense.

The Job Offer

It was time, time for Henry to sit in the limousine and drive to Rodeo Drive and time for me to join Mr. Frost and hear him talk about how unjust and mean the world had treated him. The problem with having a job at a mediocre company and having mediocre skills is the lack of power to tell your boss to shut up. As part of my discrete sucking exercise I had to listen to Mr. Frost for hours about things that didn't matter to me or anyone older than a six year old.

Henry had me beaming confidence as a person. I was feeling like I just scored an "A" on my Calculus course. Even after copying all the homework assignments from all my friends my Calculus grade had never improved. It almost took my parents donating around twenty computers before the instructor promised me a "C" if I put my name correctly on the paper.

"B.S., I want you to call me when you get out of your meeting with Mr. Frost. I want to offer you a job where you will grow as a project manager as well as enjoy working on projects that fits your personality."

I was sure Henry was joking. The only job that would fit my personality would be a job at the U.S. patent office where amongst the million pounds of paperwork I could lose just about any application and nobody would blame me. I guess that is the reason they call it "patent pending" subject to finding the original application.

"Henry, I don't know what to say? I am honored. Did you just forget that you and I had a four hour discussion? I told you everything that I didn't know about project management."

"There is a job in Japan that is waiting for you. I want you to confirm your availability. I am leading a group of over sixty project managers on a major financial project and I could use your skills as a project manager with a sense of humor. I believe your experience with the diet industry is the perfect experience I am looking for. You can help me cut down some excess fat at the company."

I realized that Henry was probably asleep when I was talking and hence only heard him talking about project management and was definitely impressed.

"Henry, you can't be serious. Japan has always been my dream city to visit every since my last visit as a kid. I would love an assignment like that. But you can't fire me for 2 years as I have no savings and unemployment is not conducive to my parents' heart."

"Consider it done. I will guarantee you employment for two years and beyond. I believe Mr. Frost is not providing you any challenge. You will enjoy your job in Japan."

The only think I knew about Japan was it had Mount Fuji and there was Saki and Sushi available everywhere. Even the Japanese version of Taco Bell was cleaner than the Four Seasons in Atlanta. I was getting excited. My parents would finally have the opportunity to include me in the family photo album.

"Henry, are you sure. I could be a liability. I could mess up your entire project single handedly. I can come up with ideas when none are needed and can have a writer's block for the entire documentation process."

"B.S., Gloria Hutchinson will call you tomorrow and give you all the details. I expect you to be at the pre-project meeting in New York within three weeks. That should give you enough time to wrap up your work at Fit-Food. Call me if you need me to talk to Mr. Frost or if he tries to sue you."

Maybe Henry was a patient of my dad, anyway he was hell bent on doing something good with my life.

I was hoping the remaining 59 snobs from Harvard would be able to handle me in Japan.

Japan the land of rising Sun was waiting for me. I could learn Karate from some real black belt and not from the criminals who parade as the local Ninja conducting classes all over the U.S.

Suddenly, I was thinking of my parents. They would be finally singing their son's praises all over the gossipy Indian community. They could also potentially inherit a large "dowry" as their son would be considered "Special Category."

I had just one last thing to think about. Passing the certification was important now. May be I could fly to some country and attempt the certification where bribing the proctor was legal.

"B.S., I almost forgot. I want you to have this. Consider it a token of our friendship."

The Mont Blanc. This was not happening to me. The bid on E-Bay would not start below three hundred.

The many good deeds my grandmother had done were finally reaping fruits for me. I knew only one Japanese word and that was "Sayonara" and now I had to learn how you ordered "Sakee."

There had to be still that one last meeting with Mr. Frost.

"Ah there you are B.S., I hope you are ready to be fired if this contract doesn't go through."

"Mr. Frost, I agree with you and I know if I fail, you will do the honorable thing and fire me immediately with a two week severance."

My grandmother had warned me about wishing for success too early in life. I could see why now.

Lightning Source UK Ltd.
Milton Keynes UK
UKHW010920271119
354284UK00002B/624/P